Fiddling

with

Socialism

Israel Helms

ISBN 9781452800370

Second Edition

Fiddling

with

Socialism

Recollections of the Future

by Israel Helms

ALSO BY ISRAEL HELMS

On Both sides of the Iron Curtain

***

This book is dedicated

to all victims

of totalitarian regimes

***

"I would rather live my life

as if there is a God,

and die to find out there isn't,

than live my life as if there isn't,

and die to find out there is."

-Reflection.

ACKNOWLEDGMENTS

I admit I had exploited my grandson Mark twice while working on this book. First, when I used him as a sounding board for my opined lecturing during our canyon-land trip. Second, when I made him read about it in my green draft. Poor young man! As if he didn't have enough in his academic and extra curriculum activity as a major in journalism and creative writing at the George Washington University. I thank you, Baby, and love you too.

I thank my editor and friend Brenda Cummings. for reading, critiquing, and joggling my manuscript, trying to preserve both some of my Russian accent in writing and an integrity of the English language being under assault.

My good friend Tom Fitzpatrick, your major in Russian history drove you into Real Estate business, not the way to get rich and powerful today, when rather ***rewriting*** the history is the way. Nevertheless, your knowledge on the subject was very instrumental. I thank you for that.

My special appreciation and best wishes to Norton Phelps, my tennis buddy, who had read first chapters of this book in process and persuaded me to follow a principle: *Less is More.*

It is wonderful to have friends like Linda Andrechyn, who is buying my books as gifts to everyone she loves, or Eileen Trueman, Ben Haney, Jim Hammond, Hank Fresch, and many others, who are open and enthusiastic about my writing and my world view. I thank you all from the bottom of my heart.

It' so good to have all my family here with me, my daughter Nora, two American born grandsons, Jacob and Mark, and my little brother Eugene, who is also retired engineer. Their support means a great deal to me.

I'd like to thank Scott Dansky for his help in processing and publication of this edition of my book.

And the last but far from the least, I'm very lucky to have on my side my friend Marina Lvovsky, who doesn't afraid to give me a little shake-up, when I drift too far to the right in my basically libertarian worldview.

CONTENTS

Israel Helms

Foreword

How to talk today's politics and love your opponent? How to dig into the darkest periods of human history and actually have fun, or at least not go crazy? This was a challenge when last summer I visited my kids and friends in New York. Like many New Yorkers, they harbored liberal worldviews; and we clashed in lively discussions. Sometimes I was saddened to see how irreconcilable our positions were, how difficult it was for all of us to stay cool. Thank Heaven, we managed to stop far short of discourse, the Russians used to find themselves in, during Bolshevik Revolution, when brother killed brother and son denounced his father, just because they had different beliefs.

As a part of the oldest generation of refugees from Soviet Russia, I've seen enough on both sides of the Iron Curtain. So, I had a chance to form my position on the choice of what political system is better to live in. In my first book[1] I had an opportunity to share my hands-on experience about different social environments. A cultural traditionalist, I reinforced my worldview on a background of liberal New England, and in the conservative environment of magnificent Arizona, where I've retired and switched from Engineering to an often less genteel sort of intellectual activity, the literal one.

So, what is the right thing for humanity—Socialism or Capitalism? How much of any is too much? This has become a topic of my reflections. A ton of books in many tongues are written on this subject; nevertheless, there is still a strong void in the public understanding of the degree of difference between these diametrically opposite systems, with drastic implications upon the life of the human race. In my conversations with Americans of different social and political affiliations during my book promotion, I was in a position to explain these differences to the listeners' satisfaction, even to their significant interest. In these exchanges I was trying to support my point of view about complicated matters in the simplest possible terms, and illustrate this point by my personal experiences from both sides of the Curtain. My listeners encouraged me to employ the spirit of these conversations

---

[1]"On both sides of the Iron Curtain."

in my second book Indeed, if some people in my new Country didn't know who Stalin was, as I learned from some of my conversations, how then can we prevent the horrible excesses of history from happening again?

*****

Let me relate to you first how one of the pre-Internet thinkers addressed the socio-political roots of this problem. Over two hundred years before the computer era, the innocent time when a writer still had to calligraphy his notes, Thomas Jefferson made a simple and very profound statement:

A government big enough to give you everything you want, is strong enough to take everything you have.

Yes, the government can often be the very root of social problems; and I would also submit—and this is based on my firsthand extensive Russian experience—that in the environment of an omnipowerful government, our very souls are on the list of goodies to be taken away as well.

Nearly a hundred years ago, the world didn't find enough intestinal fortitude to follow the words of wisdom of this great thinker and statesman. It watched a gang of radicals delude Russia into a Soviet Socialism, with Joseph Stalin as its "Messiah" and supreme leader. Then this ridiculous and very dangerous societal formation was quickly adapted—in different forms and under different guises—by Adolph Hitler in the form of National Socialism, and by many others like Mussolini, Franco, Mao, or Fidel Castro. The world refused again to realize that the pure classic Socialism they all represented fitted precisely into Jeffersonian definition of a big and omnipowerful government, seeking to free you from your independence, and to make you a hopeless slave of the system. The common instrument of governing in these systems has always been Totalitarianism, the long word with a simple meaning: *The total government control over all national means of information, production, distribution, and thereby over individual freedoms of its citizens has been its structure.* Refusing to recognize the evil nature of Socialism, the people of a Russian Empire let this system evolve and reach a stage of *perfection.* As a result, its rule cost humanity millions of lives and suffering of unimaginable proportions.

For some of the Uninformed Socialism looks and sounds quite humane and appealing but oh... so delusional. In its complete and pure form it says: *You must give everything to the state, come to your work place, and do what your conscience tells you to do; and the state will fairly and evenly distribute the national goods among its citizens.*

You don't have to worry about a thing—everything is provided.

The catch is more than obvious: Since not too many people will work without incentive or economic pressure (we are all human, after all), the state will have to suppress *your selfish, naturally capitalistic instincts* and inject *socialistic* morality, or simply, to indoctrinate you.

What if you are not receptive enough... Well, then the state will force you to work—after all it has unlimited power and leverage. Still not happy? To-o-o bad! It will inject you with a lethal dose of this morality, more than enough to send you to heaven or hell, depending on where you belong. In a pure Socialism one can't be an entrepreneur, cannot generate personal wealth, or even financial security, since security would give you some freedom and independence. These human aspirations are an absolute *No-No* in this System. The law is very clear: you are the state subject, the slave. Facing the omnipotent totalitarian state you lose your identity, and you are worth nothing— you are just a little screw in a giant bureaucratic mechanism. The process of conversion to slavery can be slow and subtle; but like in the mouth of a giant snake it's a one way street: down.

On the flip-side of this System, the empowered socialistic leaders lose any incentive to share whatever largesse the country has scrambled to produce or buy from the prosperous Capitalist, which they both hate and envy. Corruption in their ranks becomes inevitable, rampant, and out of control. The cult of personality becomes a state religion supporting a deeply corrupt system. Secret police are an instrument of unbridled oppression, a Madrassa[2] type of schooling is its education, and lousy medicine is its health care. In short, *as a socio-economic formation* it's *Socialism, as an ideology it's Communism or Fascism (depending upon what end of political spectrum it is), and as an instrument of governing it's Totalitarianism.*

Socialism and Capitalism are incompatible. The radical socialistic ideology is a destructive force for the free market. Recent example: When Senator Obama, known for his radical liberalism, was nominated to run for the presidency, the world market began a rapid decline. When he was elected, it went to a free fall. The middle class have lost half of its hard earned savings, are swamped with pink slips, and now face a prolonged economic slump.

Liberals quite often apply term *Fascist* to a seemingly harsh and disciplinarian conservatism, striving for individual responsibility and self-reliance. This misnomer comes from complete misunderstanding of the term

---

[2] Radical Muslim religious school

Fascism, which comes from Socialism by its very definition. No wonder that Hitler called his creation *The National Socialism.*"

"Can we inject a little bit of socialism into capitalism in our society?" one of my friends asked me.

"Of course," you can argue. "But watch it—it's very addictive and pervasive. Socialism does a pretty good job in keeping its guards against any capitalistic influences, while contaminating our values."

"Can we differentiate these systems in a more concise way?" he continued.

"Yes. TAX is the single term. In extreme cases, Capitalism means *no taxes*, which makes you a free individual; Socialism means *100% taxes with government handovers*, which is basic condition of dependency and slavery. Of course, in real life there is no such thing as pure and uncompromising social formation. The balance is the key.

How do different parts of the modern democratic society handle a major war of the 21st Century, the war between Capitalism and Socialism, our struggle with Neo-totalitarianism? Are there any ideological connections and tactical similarities between radical forces of different generations? What approach should the democratic forces adopt, what must they avoid to stay away from Socialism? These questions have become a focus of my reflections from a *fairly unique perspective of a Russian American of the oldest living generation.* I present it as an essay in the form of conversations between representatives of two distant age groups, between an idealistic young man and his pragmatic grandfather. The lively discussions take place on the stimulating background of the magnificent Canyons of Utah and Arizona, where we are traveling and enjoying our short time together.

The historical events in America are developing nowadays at such a meteoric pace, that even Dick Morris can hardly keep up with them in his books. My task, again, is not to compete with such thinkers in depth of reflections and the speed of reaction, but discuss some basics from a perspective of the different life experience, the basics that seem to be never going away, but still are ignored or under-estimated.

1

In the Town of Dreams

"Most of the conservatives I know, including myself, started out somewhere else on political spectrum, and evolved through time and knowledge, and experience. I personally know a single case of an individual evolving in different direction. I will leave it to Darwinists to make of that what they will."

— Burt Prelutsky:
Conservatives are from Mars; Liberals are from San Francisco.

Almost two years have passed since I've been to New York visiting my loved ones. Our political differences didn't disqualify them from being missed. Henry, one of my cultural soul mates and a former colleague, was a part of my visiting plans. I hadn't seen him for ages, and I was looking forward to a good hug. We wanted to sit together, share our thoughts, and exchange a few words about the turmoil our world has found itself in. Henry specifically wondered how the 125 deg. F. brain-melting heat in my Arizona desert had affected my "healthy sarcasm", the thing we are still in great need of in our world of absurdity. I kept asking myself all this time, how long we were going to enjoy our way of life in a Country that we, a couple of Jewish refugees from Russia, had adopted and called *Our Sweet Home*? We have found America preoccupied with a dilemma: what would it take for our Country to give in to a radical liberalism looking for Socialism of a sort, or to Islamic extremism, planning to push Shariah down our throats—whichever comes first? I was afraid that all those questions long ceased to be academic, particularly regarding my staunch metropolitan family still dwelling in their stone and glass jungle of New York, where skyscrapers often obscure the world beyond.

What makes a radical so relentless, I wondered? The picture seemed like something I'd already seen or learned before. Was it my close brush with totalitarian regime in my younger time in Russia and my obsession with historical perspectives to do with that association? Or it's indeed the legacy of the 20th Century totalitarianism we are dealing with again? I wanted to know if there is any ideological connection between Bolshevism and the modern radicalism of the West and Middle East. This seemed like a viable "scientific" problem for some nosy dilettantes in Political Science to explore.

As I expected, Henry was as furious as Glenn Beck on a TV screen. He confronted me with the same questions right from the threshold of his tiny New York apartment, bypassing all the niceties of common hospitality.

"Relax, Henry, I understand your ravings," I reasoned. "I think our thoroughly screwed-up world is hungry for some logic and common sense for a change. You know, we in Arizona are not as impulsive as you, guys, here in your *Center of the Universe*—we scratch our heads before getting mad. Any way, how are you doing? Have any troubles in dealing with your crazy traffic? I'd forgotten for a moment what it looks like… It's so good to see you again, buddy."

"I've been just fine, thanks," he responded finally. "How about you? Forgive me—I'm a terrible host. What would you like to drink? Wine? Beer? Soda? I can fix you some Shanty a nice British beer-and-sprite cocktail. It's refreshing stuff… I, myself, will have a Bloody Mary, a very bloody one—this is the mood I'm in now."

"What is on your mind, my friend? Steam out!"

"Well. I'm trying to invoke some lessons of history…and

scratching my head too," he replied. "Are you aware, Jay, what Alexander Tyler, a Scottish history professor at the University of Edinburgh, said in 1787 about fall of the ancient Athenian Republic? Some people are puzzled with his predictions nowadays. This is what he professed:

A democracy is always temporary in nature. It simply cannot exist as a permanent form of government, and it will continue to exist up until the time, when voters discover that they can vote themselves generous gifts from the public treasury. From that moment on, the majority always votes for the candidates who promise the most benefits from the public treasury, with the result that every democracy will finally collapse (due to loose policy), which is always followed by dictatorship.

The average age of the world's greatest democratic civilizations from the beginning of history has been about 200 years. During those 200 years, these nations always progressed through the following sequence:

> **-from bondage to spiritual faith;**
> **- from spiritual faith to great courage;**
> **-from courage to liberty;**
> **- from liberty to abundance;**
> **- from abundance to complacency;**

- from complacency to apathy;

-from apathy to dependency;

- from dependency back into bondage. "

"This *Bell Curve* looks pretty grim , Henri, I wish Tyler was wrong."

"Don't bet on that," he insisted. "When democracy looses its will, bondage comes back, and liberty is gradually replaced with slavery. That's when government, be it king, the financial or political oligarchy, basically the ruling minority, own everything, including your soul, and it promises to feed you like a pet...if the goodies are there, of course, which is not often the case.

The ancient Greece thinker Cicero warned us all more than two Millenniums ago. He said:

The budget should be balanced, the treasury should be refilled, public debt should be reduced, the arrogance of officialdom should be tempered and controlled, and the assistance to foreign lands should be curtailed lest Rome become bankrupt. People must again learn to work, instead of living on public assistance.

"For how long have we been talking about that already?"

"So, we are way overdue for our demise, aren't we?

"There is a really strong reason for despair, Although America was formed as a Republic *(if you can keep it,* as

13

Ben Franklin said), it is entering a phase of Democracy, which is dangerously close to anarchy with a totalitarian ruler to follow."

"How do you see the difference between Democracy and Constitutional Republic?" I asked.

"Democracy is a rule of a majority with the masses vulnerable to indoctrination. When indoctrinated, masses can support totalitarian rule of a radical minority supported by a humongous apparatus. Republic, however, is a rule of law with presumably a limited power of government. If I may be so simplistic, the totalitarian ruler would hang you, even if he knows that you are innocent; democratic mob can (oops!) hang you just to find out later and admit that you are guiltless; the good Republic can also hang you—however very reluctantly—but only if you were proven to be guilty by the due process. As you can see the difference is profound."

"So where are we now?"

"I'm afraid, the United States is pretty close to the bottom; and some people here, in our America, can't wait to see this cycle complete. Nothing would probably make European socialists happier than the failure of American capitalism."

"What are you suggesting, Henry?" I was still trying to play devil's advocate.

14

"I suggest we'd better start packing our bags for a long trip, say…to Mars or to a hidden part of the Moon, if we let this slide continue."

"There is another danger looming over our way of life," I echoed. "As Professor Bernard Lewis, the world-renowned Middle Eastern and Islamic scholar, has indicated:

Islam could soon be the dominant force in Europe, which, in the name of political correctness, has abdicated the battle for cultural and religious control. Europeans are losing their own loyalties and their self-confidence. They have no respect for their own culture and have surrendered on every issue regarding Islam, in a mood of self-abasement and multi-culturalism'."

"Here you are. I hate to sound redundant, Jay—we are already pretty numb hearing about our troubles every day; but the attacks on our Republic from two fronts is a matter of our very survival. I don't think we can afford to loose sight of reality even for a moment. Let me briefly outline our dilemma, if I may. I'll try to be pithy. I've been thinking about this for quite some time; and I need to hear your opinion." He reached for his notebook:

"First and very basic: we are fighting a relentless and dangerous enemy, a bunch of crazies, who would use *any means available today not just to kill us, but completely*

15

erase our Western civilization. They are ready to die for their coveted rewards in the other world. In short – we are at war.

Second: America is practically alone in this fight—don't tell me that our diplomats didn't make enough effort. We can count neither on a totally corrupted and heavily socialistic United Nations, nor on our 'friends', whom we liberated from the bloody Nazis and fed when they were hungry.

Third: the open borders, liberal criminal laws and lawyers, and corrupt politicians are greatly undermining our national security. It makes our Country vulnerable to different sorts of unimaginable enemy attacks.

Forth: during the entire century of our confrontation with communism and Islamic Jihad, however preposterous it may sound, we've been facing an odd phenomenon. In times of sharp political and especially military confrontation of our Country with enemy, when a citizen's loyalty is vital, sizable groups of vocal individuals could become very active in undermining the well justified American defensive effort, and put our defenders of the front line at risk. Where are the noisemakers at this point with our obvious progress in Iraq? I know where they are. They are sitting silent somewhere with their tongues (pardon my French) deep in their 'mufflers', recycling their own crap, and waiting for the next opportunity to release their stench over again.

Last but not the least: minority of radicals often owns a quiet majority of goodhearted moderates. They have been quite successful in selling their radical propaganda.

It's ironic that American cultural traditionalists dwelling mostly in sparsely populated Red States and therefore the least vulnerable to the mass terror, are the most concerned and vigilant about fighting Islamic Jihad. They bend over backwards to convince a majority of liberals, that in the case of a terrorist attack, the dwellers of metropolitan cities would suffer the most."

"I liked your *French*—no Russian accent there," I chuckled. "Besides, I've been wondering about this phenomenon, too... You may find it far-fetched, but the more I think about this, the more similarities I find between the Bolshevik dogma of Leon Trotsky's Permanent Revolution and the Wacko stand of today's radical Left—the same ideology, the same delusional zeal."

"What do you mean?" Henry cried with made-up surprise. "That seems like a really radical thought?"

"It may seem so, but I believe there's a lot of truth in it. You and I lived through Stalinism, and endured its environment first hand. We know what it entails. The

'Fifth Column' in Russia, represented by a relatively small group of zealots, destabilized their own Country's young democracy and became a hummer in totalitarian takeover. They prepared their Country for defeat by undermining its immune system and, perhaps not always intentionally, played right into the hands of totalitarian forces. Trotskyites of the Bolshevik Revolution left their grim self-defeating legacy and directives for some modern zealots to follow and to fall into the same trap."

"You're right, buddy." Henry agreed. "The radicals of all times and colors share a common goal to defeat natural human instinct for freedom and self-reliance, build humongous bureaucratic apparatus, concentrate all resources in the hands of the elite, and make people complacent and dependent upon government alms. In Stalinist Russia, for instance, we couldn't even have a checking account or credit of any sort. Neither could we change our residence from one city to another without special *propiska*[3], which would deliberately take forever to obtain. These methods were effective elements of the state economic and psychological domination over each and every individual. When totalitarian transformation was complete, Stalin didn't need Trotsky any more. Totalitarian

---

[3] Special permission, *russ*

regime doesn't need an *idealism* of the original revolutionaries. They are inconvenient in building a new society, the society of an ultimate cynicism."

"I like your logic, Henry. I'd love to exploit it in a new book. What is obvious to us, is not necessarily an axiom to others. We're not political scientists by any means, but what the heck—everyone is writing books today. Just like in the first book, our writing will perhaps be easily recognized by our Russian accent, something that we will never get rid of. So what? We have something else: *We've been there; and not too many people around can tell this story with the passion of the long life experience.*"

"I would let readers visit the minds of the radical Left of different generations, but the not so distant historical periods. We want him to understand the mechanism of their destructive drive to socialism. If we can manage to elevate the public interest to some of these questions, I would consider this effort worth it... Wait a minute, Henry." My mind was reeling. "I have an idea. I know it is always helpful to test the major points of a new book on a good intelligent listener before you even start it."

"Maybe, Jay, you can find somebody from the radical Left as a devil's advocate," he advised.

"Oh... No, Henry! He'll ruin my stomach. I have a perfect candidate; it's my grandson Myron. He is a major now at the George Washington University in DC, taking journalism, political science and other good stuff. He is perfect in every sense--I believe he's a good liberal. I'll take him on a spectacular tour around southern Utah and northern Arizona. He may also be very instrumental in balancing out the Russian accent in my writing... Well, I'm long done with my Shanty, and it was pretty good. What else do you have in your *wonder-bar?*" I felt a new wave of excitement.

"Help yourself, be my guest. There is some shanty left." He pointed toward the bar.

"Talking about the sinister effect of unlimited power of the state on society," he inquired with a great deal of sarcasm. "Tell me why Gore is so obsessed with his worldwide environmentalist campaign to spend trillions for something science is not quite sure about. Some scientists, as you know, see Arctic cups melting, the others –Antarctic ice fields thickening; while some see a common cycle, the others – a trend."

"Maybe the coming Ice Age is a sign of global warming?" I suggested.

"That's exactly what they say," he said, matching my sarcasm.

"Why do you think Al Gore is so adamant about that?" I asked him.

"You tell me."

"Think, my friend, about the vast power he would control by the amount of funds on hand? It's the wildest fantasy of every ultra-liberal wacko. Stalin and Bin Laden could only dream about this kind of opportunity. Besides, who likes to admit his complete fiasco in the middle of a crusade he instigated. Had Newt Gingrich offered this project, I would probably have different vibes. The issue largely is not what to do, but how to do it. Where is our Gipper, that tall handsome cowboy in a broad white hat? Don't you think we need him again?"

"So, you don't trust our brilliant inventor of internet, do you?"

"Well. Not yet, Henry. Gore just got his Nobel Prize, and joined Kofi Annan and Yasser Arafat on the Walk of the Fame. Watch for his next move. Do you think it could be something like scaling down his energy-hungry life style? I doubt it."

"You don't think Gore is the right guy to even touch this kind of project, do you?" he repeated and chuckled.

"Not until he at least matches his rhetoric with a good personal example. What would be wrong with Gore living in a nice 2000 square foot house in a gated community like mine in the Colorado River Valley of Arizona?" I proposed. "The property would have a little Casita for the guards to use—Gore is entitled to some security as a former high-level government official. The house would be equipped with all the energy saving gadgets he could buy or invent. The year-around tennis and biking would also be very good for his health and for the environment. Group visitor gatherings could be accommodated in the roomy and well-equipped communal clubhouse, with First Class tickets on commercial flights available in a minute. Online conferencing would connect him with an audience all over the world; and on top of all that luxury - the insurance and taxes are low; fruits and vegetables are fresh and available year round with the Safeway supermarket around the corner. In overall, I think he could live quite a comfortable, exemplary, and very productive life, polluting no air, no water, and no people around him-- and all of that at a tiny fraction of his current energy consumption. This would be a real demo of leadership."

"You've figured it all out, Jay," Henry replied with a sigh of relief. "I couldn't catch my breath while you were counting all this largesse. By living such an environmentally kosher life Al would perhaps justify his *Noble Prize and all his Hollywood awards.*"

"At least nobody would call him *a Hypocrite.*"

$$*****$$

22

...The day following my conversation with Henry, I called Myron and invited him to visit me in my Colorado River Valley retreat.

"Sorry, Deda[4], you know how much I want to see you," Myron apologized, "I don't think I can do it right now. I'll call, though, to update you about my schedule."

---

[4] Grandfather, *russ*

2

Rebel in Exile

"Trotsky's idea of Permanent Revolution will always be attractive to the kind of romantic who believes that he is being oppressed by global capitalism when he maxes out his credit card.."

-Clive James: *Leon Trotsky.*

Leon Trotsky was the guy I wanted to talk to Myron about. What does Myron's generation know about him? Who was this man, what was his legacy, considering our current fight with radical liberalism? Was he just a ruthless and delusional egomaniac and mass murderer who lost his fight to a wilier player, Joseph Stalin, or a thinker, as some insisted, and a tribune blessed with eloquence, goodness, and a spirit, who had just made a mistake and sacrificed his talent, inspiration, and life itself. Was he a freedom fighter or an idiot chasing that *utopian firebird called*

Communism, the ideology of totalitarian paradise on earth, mandatory for everyone in sight ...or else! Stalin used him, stripped him naked, raped, and threw him out in the cold. Was it just bad luck or a matter of iron logic?

Since its introduction by Karl Marx as a theory, the idea of Communism has been imposed on billions of people around the globe, leaving behind the terrible legacy of horror, physical destruction, and moral abuse. This ideology has even left to it's followers *The Communist Manifesto,* one of its "Holy Books", a detailed school of ideas and actions for the future warlords of terrorism, brutal dictators, and criminals against humanity.

Leon Trotsky, the *creative* Marxist, made this idea his lifetime obsession. Without his effort, the Bolshevik Revolution wouldn't have survived the massive onslaught of its enemies, domestic and foreign, from the very beginning of the Civil War. He was a "CEO" as well as the most prominent scapegoat of the Bolshevik revolution, when the time came for this utopist to surrender his power to the ruthless dictator.

In any case, without Trotsky's grim legacy, our book wouldn't have an opportunity of harvesting this fertile field. Without this zealot, your obedient servant would probably continue to quietly practice his Engineering profession in Russia. Quite possibly, he would have never written in English and would have remained in Moscow, committed to his native Russian, the tongue of Pushkin and Tolstoy. Instead, with Trotsky's critical help, almost the entire 20th Century slid into an abyss of totalitarian ideology. Without his legacy of Permanent Revolution as a rule of radical minority over the complacent majority, a legacy which is still alive and well, humanity would probably have never lived through the many horrible wars and atrocities of the last Century. This was my test of intelligence I wanted to impose on my young guest.

*****

The steamer *Il'yich* was put to steam by an urgent order. One of two major originators and players in the October Revolution, Leon Trotsky, arrived in Odessa by the train on the night of February 10, 1929. He looked through the car window at a familiar place—he had spent seven years of his school life in this city. Their car was brought right to the steamer. It was bitterly cold. Despite the late hour, troops and agents of the OGPU[1] surrounded the pier. Here he had to say good-by to his younger son and daughter-in-law, to never see them again.

---

[1] Soviet Secret Police, the early version of KGB

The *Ilyich* carried no cargo or other passengers but Leon Trotsky, his wife, the life long comrade, Natalia Sedova, and also his older son Liova, who spent a year of exile with his father on the Chinese frontier. It took off about one o'clock in the morning. For a distance of sixty miles the icebreaker helped to make a passage for them. The gale that had raged for a few days caught them here on its last effort.

On February 12 they entered the Bosporus. Turkish police boarded the steamer at Buyukdere to check off the passengers, and Trotsky handed the following statement for transmission to the President of the Turkish Republic, Kemal Pasha:

"Dear Sir: At the gate of Constantinople, I have the honor to inform you that I have arrived at the Turkish frontier not of my own choice, and that I will cross this frontier only by submitting to force. I request you, Mr. President, to accept my appropriate sentiments: L. Trotsky. February 12, 1929."

After spending a few days in the Russian Consulate the family was placed in a small apartment on the outskirts of Constantinople and left to their fate. Trotsky could count his blessings. He wasn't killed somewhere in the dark dungeons of OGPU—Trotsky was too big, too popular for that, and his followers were too numerous and too restless.

This man of giant intellect, the passionate writer, speaker, and ruthless revolutionary was admired by his comrades almost as much as being cautiously respected by his enemies in Russia and abroad. He was huge while being persuasive and even bigger, when he was wrong. His lifelong mania was liberation of the Working Class through world wide "Permanent Revolution". Capitalism at that point of industrial revolution had laid a socio-economic foundation of the current Western world, but in the process it was not very kind to the proletariat and generated strong revolutionary opposition. Bolsheviks exploited this situation. Stalin was careful but determined about his dealings with Trotsky and had no choice but to grant his major competitor some temporary gift of life.

Now, Leon Trotsky, this notorious rebel, had to find a country willing to give him asylum at the time of a deep retreat of international proletarian revolutionary sentiments.

Trotsky applied for asylum in Germany, Netherlands, France, and England. Nobody wanted to take the notorious rebel. Even permission for temporary medical visits with the doctors who had been observing him during his previous exiles by Russian Czar, were denied. Trotsky joked: "This meant that I could appreciate the full advantages of democracy only as a corpse". In the mean time, he had plenty of opportunity to look back and reflect on his turbulent life.

The greatest irony of Trotsky's wasted life was complete disconnection of his ideas from human reality. His desperate effort to create and build a stable social structure without checks and balances was destined to be as futile as an attempt to make a mechanical robot work without a control system. The only way to keep this structure manageable was an application of brutal force. For that simple task the coming totalitarian ruler didn't need a brilliant fool, a noisy and highly inconvenient idealist. So, Trotsky was by the nature of things destined for demise and disposal. When he was thrown away, nobody in their right mind dared to pick the troublemaker up from the heap of history, where he belonged. Killed by Stalin's assassin in 1940, he now observes the ill fate of his life-long revolutionary effort from *the other world*, the place which existence he'd flatly denied.

3

Test Bed of Bolshevism

"Mr. Khmelinsky?" the counter attendant asked me, when I returned to the hotel after a busy day on my engineering service trip to Palo Alto.

"Yes, ma'am."

"Your grandson Myron left a message for you to call him."

"Thank you very much..."

"I couldn't reach you, Deda," Myron answered the phone. "Is everything alright?"

"Yes. It was a hectic conference, and I had to turn my cell phone off. It's over now; I'm heading home. What's up kiddo?"

"I told you I couldn't come. Well, I have about a week and a half after all. So, I'm coming, if you don't mind. I think I have a constitutional right to see my Deda before I fly away to school, don't I?"

"Terrific! Of course you have. I'll pick you up at the Las Vegas airport, and we'll take a nice trip around Southern Utah and Northern Arizona. I'll show you our National Parks, a Garden of Eden that the Masters of Renaissance didn't have a chance to see. Bring your fancy camera with you. You'll see places you'll never forget, views that will humble your soul and lift your spirit. Besides, I've missed you; and I also need you as a devil's advocate."

"I missed you too, terribly. What are you up to?"

"You'll see..."

Myron arrived in Vegas on one of the hottest days of the year. We skipped the entertainments of Sin City and took off north to Utah. Destination – canyons.

*****

"Where do you consider yourself on a political spectrum at this particular moment in your life?" I asked Myron, when we pulled out of the airport garage. "You're moving fresh to the campus of George Washington University. GW is a pretty liberal school. Are you planning to blend in, or have your own voice? When you interviewed your guests as a host of your high school radio show, did you feel any sentiments toward a particular political philosophy?"

"I felt some sentiments towards personalities that I liked or disliked, but I don't think I was coming to the interview in a prejudicial mood, Deda."

"Good! This will help... You were very busy in high school, involved in many activities. You liked it, didn't you?"

"I liked all of it—communications, politics, art, music, singing. I loved acting, writing and competitive tennis. It was an experience, and an amazing one. I'm hoping to get some of that at GW. I think I'll try political science and communication, maybe journalism and creative writing. Have you read my school essays, Deda?"

"Yes, I have—both the essays and the poems. They were getting progressively more mature with you taking the course in Creative Writing."

"Thanks, Deda. I do feel like I'm gaining more confidence in communication and writing... but I suppose you wanted to see me not for all these questions you could well ask over the phone or even Skype."

"That's correct. You see, we want to collect material for our second book, a sequel. As you know, I happened to be the main character of the first one, *On Both Sides of the Iron Curtain*. I was born the year of the great famine, the result of the first major failure of communism. I grew up in the pre-war Soviet Union, went through WWII time, witnessed the whole cycle of atrocities of this totalitarian system, and before its disintegration immigrated with my daughter and son-in law (your parents) to the United States, where you were born. You know most of it: you were part of this story.

The first book, essentially semi-biographical, showed our life against the background of a lifetime development of Socialism. We didn't touch the subject of its creation, early evolution, and its influences on our life here in the West. I'd like to fill up some of these gaps and expand our story to a new somewhat more polemical level, if I may. I believe that our life time experiences on both sides of an ideological divide and our curiosity can be instrumental in the search for logical connections between different forms of totalitarian regimes. Our focus will be on critical differences between totalitarianism and our Republic of Law. Ben Franklin, as you probably know, warned us about a vulnerability of the latter and the diabolic appeal of the former."

"Do you think, Deda, we may experience oppression of the same degree of evil as Nazism and Stalinism again?"

"If we let it happen. Why do you think the current administration is in such a hurry creating a mysterious new government within government? Why a majority of

33

important decisions are discussed and made in total secrecy?

I think totalitarian regime normally comes to power with the help of certain, seemingly benign political movements within society. These movements, more idealistic than realistic, don't pass the test of time. They are often falling victims of demagoguery and exploited by unscrupulous and ambitious leaders. In fact, this was how Stalinism evolved from the radical Left movement, fostered and materialized by Lenin and Trotsky."

"I admit, Trotsky's connection was somewhat missing in my understanding of the Bolshevik revolution."

"Well, look around, Myron. Bad historical cycles show its ugly teeth again, and again there seems to be some similarity in forces involved in the process. If this connection is real, our second book would have a chance to say something useful about how to recognize such forces, and help to keep them away. I came out with an idea of testing some of the major points of this book on somebody smart, intelligent, and open-minded, to use someone as a devil's advocate, so to speak; and I can't see anyone better than you, young man, for this task."

"Are you serious? I'm flattered, Deda!"

"Yes, Myron, I am serious, and I'm suggesting the following format. We'll take a nice tour around a magnificent American West, including Zion, Bryce, Glenn, and Grand Canyons; then we'll go south to Sedona, so called the 'Spiritual Center' of Arizona; and then we'll head west to Colorado River Valley where I live. Traveling along, we'll have plenty of time to discuss our questions in a form of free exchanges of opinion. There will be no limitation in the character of the questions, but we'll have to stick with the topic as close as possible. Weather is great, expenses are paid...by your Deda. What can go wrong? On top of my obvious desire to see you, Baby, this was the reason why I called you. I need your help. See, intelligence begets its perks and obligations. I need you not just for your intelligence, but also your common sense; not just your sensitivity, but also your character. You know very well that these qualities don't always come together. There are a lot of 'intelligent' pinheads roaming around the world. Nazis were very good in shedding tears in opera and concert halls before going back to Gestapo quarters for the next round of atrocities... So, what do you think?"

"Wow, Deda, I don't know what to say. I do have plenty of questions. This is a huge task, but it sounds great."

"Well, ask away. Just don't miss the incredible views along our route."

"Okay, you mentioned 'Intelligent Pinheads' in quite derogatory manner. I hope to gain my intelligence some day. You are holding Doctorate degree and have been designing Intelligent Machines. For Pete sakes, you are even writing books now! To what category of 'heads' do we belong?"

"Hey, take it easy, buddy. Higher education doesn't necessarily mean high intelligence or high integrity. Don't you agree? There are plenty of highly educated people roaming around who confuse education with common sense. They're convinced that reading a few books makes them capable of running a complex business or government operation; or that interviewing a dozen Pop Stars makes them highly qualified political commentators. Worst of all, some of them are using their diplomas as a Certificate of Power. They teach farmers what crops to raise, the industrial executives – what cars to build, and the teachers – how to interpret and present historical events as it fits into their theory. This is exactly what happened, when the Russian revolutionary elite took power over a gigantic and immensely complex country, and brought the bread basket of the world to deadly famine. In the process they killed new democracy in its cradle."

"What a relief, Deda! At least you used words *some* and *plenty.*"

"I hope you are not getting bored!"

"I, Deda, have always been curious about the evolution of

36

the liberal movement in Russia. What kept Russia as such a backward Country for so long?"

"Well Myron, this subject is a fascinating one on its own merit, and it has already produced a score of good books. If you wish, I can touch on it briefly."

"Please do... Why, for example, couldn't the Russian democracy take hold when its Czar was overturned and a democratic Provisional Government was established?"

"We have to start from the ancient times. Are you ready for some digging?"

"I love archeology."

"Good, me too, but don't mean picks and shovels. You're probably already familiar with some fragments of Russian history, but I want to put it in perspective for you.. We can start from the field of science called Genetics, a term very popular now at any level, including the kitchens and bedrooms of ordinary citizens."

"Genetics?"

"Yes. Simply speaking, the process of adaptation and mutation is nothing else then saving useful information and acting upon it. Every new generation develops an ever increasing ability to favor this useful information and slowly modifies its genetic code for the sake of comfort and survival."

"Hmm...The *useful* one?"

"Sure, think about that. It just feels more comfortable. Don't you try to act upon this principle yourself? This ability to favor and save positive information allows every given species to move up in its evolution... Is it getting too 'scientific'?"

"No, Deda. This kind of 'popular biology' I can handle. I am with you so far. Go on..."

"Any way, no specie, in accordance with theory of Evolution, would survive without this drive and ability of self-improvement. This process worked in every single case including the primates, so what they say, and... it faltered on humans."

"Why is that?"

"Because humans very often make much less sense than amebas, those single cell creatures seen only under the microscope; and this in spite of apparent favors humans have always been receiving from Nature."

"What have they done that's so bad, Deda?"

"Humans have done and still do a lot of good things— don't get me wrong: They invented the wheel, including the steering one you wiggle while driving your car. They learned how to start fire and to rotisserie the mammoth's prime ribs on it. They developed different tools, from stone wedges to the space robotic manipulators. They like the comfort, just as those amebas; but unlike the single cell primitives they have a distinct addiction to self-destruction. They abuse themselves physically with all forms of harmful substances, as well as socially, by listening to the unscrupulous demagoguery of their political leaders and media pundits. They even act upon this demagogery, and form long lasting cultural habits, detrimental to themselves and their neighbors. Like a few other species, humans kill even when they are not hungry, just for the pleasure. Think, Myron, how low we have sunk."

"I know it's depressing, but how much has all this colorful science to do with Russian history and the Bolshevik Revolution?"

"More than you think, I guess. Please bear with me. I am trying to answer the question why this revolution took place in Russia, and why Russia was a perfect platform for totalitarianism, but not the Western developed world, as Karl Marx desperately professed."

"All right; go ahead."

"You, Myron, have been in Russia a few times visiting your grandmother. But you've seen only Moscow and its pretty shabby suburbs haven't you?"

"Yes, I wanted to visit St. Petersburg; this amazing classic European city that I saw in pictures, so different from the medieval downtown of Moscow; but I didn't have an opportunity."

"I do love that city, Myron, but St. Petersburg and to a lesser degree Moscow doesn't represent Russia, just like New York City and San Francisco, in different ways, don't represent America. Let's take a quick look at this infinitely rich and miserably poor Country of Russia from a historical point of view."

"I don't think Americans understand it."

"I agree. Russia was self-isolated from the world for a thousand years. The history books indicate that at the beginning of the second millennium AC, one thousand years ago, the great Eurasian plane (the Eastern Europe and Siberia up to the Pacific Ocean) was dominated by the vast Asiatic empires - Iranian, Turkish, Mongolian, etc. As the last of them melted away, Muscovy, the young Slavic city-state in Eastern Europe, expanded steadily through several centuries until it became the largest continuous land empire in the world. It spread over endless forests and grasslands, sparsely settled by nomadic tribes. Everything was there for a great nation to survive and relax. By the time of the Bolshevik revolution the empire of Czars sprawled across two continents from the Gulf of Finland in the West to the Pacific Ocean, from the frozen Arctic Ocean in the North to hot desert sands and semi-tropical mountain slopes bordering the whole southern half of

Asia. History had no parallels to such vastness. The Russian empire embraced 8,500,000 square miles of territory—one sixth of the total land surface of the globe, with one tenth of the human race. Just a Russian European part was equal to the whole lands of Western Europe. Two thirds of the empire's bulk laid on the outskirts of the continent, a fabulously rich in natural resources but hardly accessible Asiatic tundra and steppe[1]."

"It's amazing, Deda. I knew it was big but this picture is mind-boggling. It explains why Russia could be invaded, but never defeated."

"Exactly! This is one of the points I'm trying to make. Against every powerful invader the chief defenders of this open plain have always been distance, mud and winter— not socialism, not state property, not the Five-Year plan, and not even Stalin's military genius, as the communist propaganda maintained for three quarters of a century. Winning tactics have always been the age-old strategy of a *Scorched Earth*. This combination worked against Hindenburg and Hitler in the 20th century, against Napoleon in the 19th, Charles XII of Sweden in the 18th and against many others. The inventors of this strategy were Scythians, ancient Slavs, who kicked out Darius the

---

[1] Grasslands

41

Great of Persia in 512 BC. Scythians, the inhabitants of what is now Ukraine, would retreat inland, driving away their cattle, burning grasslands and poisoning the wells. They drew the Darius' forces deep into scorched land and then counter-attacked. By weakening Darius in the process, they, ironically, helped to save the already conquered Greece, of which Scythians had never heard. The Czar's armies on the Eastern front saved Paris in 1914, and the Red Army, by resisting German invasion, saved London in WWII. Even heroic Spartans and Greece's treacherous mountain passes couldn't do a better job against Darius, than the Russian wilderness. In fact, by saving Greece, the Russians two and a half millennia ago had preserved the first European Democracy, the political prototype of the Western civilization. Isn't that a funny paradox?"

"This is fascinating. So, as I understand, as soon as Hitler's offence in Russia faltered, his fate was sealed."

"I think his doom was sealed from the beginning, when he made his dumb decision to start the war."

"Do you think Hitler would have lost even if he had captured Leningrad and Moscow?"

"I think so. That's what history shows. Russians know how to conduct the scorch land operations... In the aftermath of WWII, Russia continued its expansion, bringing the western borders of its empire well into Central Europe."

"Not any more"

"You are correct. The expansionism carried powerful long-term side effects. The inferiority in land mass and natural resources helped the West to develop cultural and technological superiority. Russia, in the mean time, relied on its vastness and invincibility and rested on its laurels."

"So, it seems like Russia was a sick giant by the time of the 1917 Bolshevik revolution. Still, why, Deda, didn't this revolution happen somewhere else in Western Europe?"

"You can answer this question yourself. Just take a look at capitalism in developed countries at their peak in the second half of the last century. The Industrial Revolution had stabilized. New revolution, the technological one, greatly stimulated a free enterprise and the global trade offered by a democratic system of capitalism. The working class, to a large extent, became part of the system, the lower echelon of the middle class, basically protected by some corporate and governmental provisions much better than at the onset of the industrial revolution and the times of sweatshops. Of course the rich and poor were still there, but I haven't seen any radicalism among workers, only among some of their leaders, often with questionable self-serving agendas. Karl Marx was teaching his followers that communism had the best chance to win in the highly developed capitalistic countries, where the proletariat was supposed to be the strongest. He was dead wrong. On the contrary, totalitarianism feeds on ignorance and backwardness, on defeat and isolation. It happened in Russia badly beaten by Japan, and in Germany, when they were defeated and humiliated in WWI. Nazism came to power in Germany on the shoulders of the failed capitalism. It established National Socialism, the system with the same premise as Bolshevism: The State against an Individual."

"This was an interesting excursion."

"So, tell me, Myron, what conclusion would you draw from this history lesson?"

"I think the warning point you're trying to make is for the people enjoying their life in the West but craving socialism."

"Well. It was true for Russia in the time of the Bolshevik Revolution. Things have changed rapidly. Remember the Tyler's Bell curve? The enablers of the neo-totalitarianism can stay home in the West now—there is plenty of *progressive* work for them to do on the sliding slope of our democracy. This is what we have to keep in mind. The Bolshevik revolution took place at the beginning of an era of prosperity in the bourgeois democracy. This I know from history and what is currently becoming a history. Do you know what stage of democracy we find ourselves at on the Tyler's scale... if we don't keep our Republic as Franklin warned?"

"Are you eluding, Deda, that we are at the low end of the slide?"

"Yes, sadly so, and Professor Tyler wouldn't be too happy about that. Now we have no choice but to shake our lethargy off and answer a fundamental question: what is causing this decline of our Republic; and first of all, ask ourselves what it will take to stop it.

Glenn Beck in his comments on the Hitler assassination attempt at the end of the WWII stressed how blind, complacent, and impotent were the world leaders to deal with coming fascism:

At what point did people say: Gee, now it's too late? How many people were willing to step gladly up to the table to topple that regime but only when they thought they were winning? If it didn't look like they were going to win, they were on the other side... I'm against you, unless you're winning. Then I'm for you."

"It's a pretty frightening reality. It often gives the villain a free hand. I wouldn't mind talking about this in more detail, Deda."

"Well, buckle up, my friend."

*****

The conversation made our travel from Las Vegas to Zion National Park pass in the blink of an eye. We followed scenic Route 167 along the North-Western Rim of Lake Mead, and then joined Highway 16 North to Utah. We entered Southern Zion via Mount Carmel Highway; proceeded through the Canyon with its spectacular gorges; passed gigantic stone masses of the West Temple and Watch Guard, and the breathtaking half-mile chasm of the Virgin River. We climbed the spiral slope of the Pine Creek Canyon with unbelievable views, passed through the Zion Tunnel with arches and windows. We were speechless for a change. In the late afternoon the descending sun changed the colors of the rock formations by the minute. The air was crisp and fresh.

We exited Zion in dusk and followed toward Bryce Canyon. Life was wonderful, far away from the world's problems…but we still had some work to do.

"Talking about *Zion* Canyon reminded me of something I wanted to learn," Myron asked me when we pulled onto the highway. "What was the level of Jewish participation in the Bolshevik Revolution? Was it really disproportionate to the general population, as some people insist?"

"Well, taken out of historical context it would seem like it was. In short (and I don't care much about political correctness), the initial intention of the Russian radical Left, although utopist, could be considered honorable in a way—they were fighting for the liberation of Russia from a Czarist absolutism and against the quite abusive at that point young and wild capitalism, which they were not able to project to the future and appreciate. Jews have actively participated in political activity, partially due to some specific historical and cultural conditions in Russia; but the overwhelming majority of them belonged to Mensheviks, Populists, Jewish Bund and other factions of the liberal social democratic movement, which were opposed to Bolsheviks, the party of the radical Left. Moreover, Stalin had eliminated practically all Jews in party leadership, along with their families, when he learned that some of them were in direct or even potential opposition to his policies. He spared just one, Lasar Kaganovich, the perpetual figurehead, the father of his mistress, and the 'yes man' of no opinion. Stalin was a Mafioso with mentality of a hit man.

I remember at the peak of Stalin's murderous campaign

against Jewish medical doctors and scientists Soviet Jews prayed for Lasar Kaganovich. 'Lasar won't let us down, he is a good man' they kept crying. We can see now how pathetic was their plea. "

"Why, Deda, was the Jewish population so involved in the Social Democratic movements in general?"

"You see, our intellectual makeup, just like in many other ethnic groups, is a unique product of history. There are two schools of thought about why we are so different. One claim is a divine origin of *People of the Book*, a people ordained to symbolize and expose the best and brightest as well as the questionable characteristics of our human race. I think, quite often we've been almost like a punching bag for God's frustration with humanity, if I may be so terribly profane.

The other, more secular school teaches that Jews by pure chance got their hands on the Book, something they could read and argue about, and get educated before anybody else could. The education gave them some power of survival in an often hostile environment, the ability to solve their problems in exile through knowledge and negotiations.

Every practicing Jew is his own Rabbi, you know. In the way, he is addressing the Torah and its Giver directly without a middleman. The tradition of analysis and interpretation of every written word made us a bunch of stubborn and opinionated Yentls and relentless truth seekers, sometimes to the point of obsession or even absurdity, if you will. We are not known much for physical or chemical substance abuse in or outside the family. Unless blatantly provoked, a Jew would rarely harm you, but he would sure debate you to death, if he feels he's right. Look at the massive Jewish participation in the liberal movement today. Just like Leon Trotsky, many of us think that our mission in life is to cleanse capitalism from its 'unfair' traits, or even eliminate it all together. Often enough in this complex process we step right into dung, looking for socialism as a solution... Don't stare at me like that, with your handsome Hebrew eyes!"

"You make me blush like a girl, Deda"

"You have a gentle heart of a girl... But let's come back to your theme. When Jews were expelled from Palestine and dispersed all over the world, they had no land, no physical power, nothing to work with, but only their literacy, knowledge and drive. While ancestors of the so celebrated Aryans of the future Third Reich still ate their royal meals without utensils, Jews were working hard on perfecting the Text Book of mass education in philosophy, science and medicine, called *the Talmud*, and on setting the groundwork of modern Western mysticism and spiritualism, and that by the way, is something the emerging Western civilization liked so much, that it was put into the foundation of its Judeo-Christian philosophy.

In the course of centuries Jews migrated from one country to another, educated local rulers, got promoted, and became wealthier. Then they were robbed when it was convenient, massacred and expelled—it's always so tempting to kick a butt of a powerless victim, especially if he has a couple of guldens in his pocket. Jews migrated through Northern Africa, Spain, France, Germany, Poland, and dead-ended on the fringes of Western Russia, Ukraine, Lithuania and Eastern Poland.

Up to the eighteenth century, when Jewish refugees showed up on the Western horizon, the Ukraine was a Russian borderland. Only at the century's end, with the defeat of the Turks and the partition of Poland, did Moscow's power expand through Ukraine to the shores of the Black Sea. The annexation of Ukraine, Poland and Baltic shores brought to the empire a considerable number of Jewish subjects, the largest and densest concentration of Jews in the world. They were desperately poor, making their living mostly as innkeepers, petty merchants and artisans.

The 19th Century, however, presented some relief for the Jewish ghetto. In 1804, the Russian emperor Alexander opened a new avenue of escape out of the economic noose steadily tightening about Jewish settlers. He offered state lands in the so-called 'Russia Minor', the sparsely populated provinces of Ukraine, for Jewish agricultural colonization. For the first time in the course of history, driving Jews out of agriculture promised suddenly to be reversed.

Alexander's brother Nicolas continued the Alexandrine policy. He allowed Jews to serve in the army for 25 years, and after that to take up new lands and settle in new villages in the middle of the grasslands. At the same time he allowed Jewish youth to have some traditional education in a few major cities. Jews took advantage of it and quickly formed a new solid class of intelligentsia—the hunger for education was solidly encoded in our genes by centuries of evolution. When Alexander II reversed this policy in 1872, the Genie was already out of the bottle. In 1882 the radical anarchistic group Narodnaya Volya[1] assassinated Alexander II. A few members of this group were Jews. New ukas[2] forbade Jews to rent, lease or buy land any longer. The noose was tightening again; but freedom, even an embryonic one, is too precious to give

---

[1] *Will of the People*, russ.

[2] *Directive*, russ.

up easily. That was the beginning of the Marxist Social Democratic movement in Russia. Vladimir Lenin, a ruthless and determined revolutionary theoretician, the believer in *liberation* of masses through the most aggressive militant form of Marxism, took the lead. He was obviously a talented, charismatic, and pragmatic politician. He always maintained working relationships with his philosophical and tactical opponents - the *Mensheviks, Populists, Bundists, Economists, and also with the Liberal and Bourgeois Democrats.* He knew everyone's abilities and their weak points, and he tried to keep in mind how close to the state controlling elite he could safely allow any one to be. He realized that the socialist state by its very nature would require a monumental bureaucratic government with lots of educated foot soldiers. Lenin considered Leon Trotsky exceptionally talented and capable revolutionist, his primary successor, and he warned about Stalin's totalitarian tendencies. Sure, had he lived longer, he would have had plenty of opportunity to learn that *totalitarianism is a very basic attribute of socialism; one can't exist without the other.*"

"Amazing and pretty heavy stuff; I am beat, Deda. You wore me out. Let's continue tomorrow." Myron stretched and hugged me.

XXXXX

After checking into a rustic hotel minutes away from Bryce Canyon National Park and settling in our room we stepped out of the lodge for a few minutes. It was almost a full moon and the night was beautiful.

"Good to be away for awhile from the busy world," Myron said. "Thank you for having me here."

"Tomorrow, Myron, I'll show you the real beauty, something I've never forgotten, since I saw it for the first time 15 years ago"

4

Something is brewing

Between elections, the party leaders were supreme, and any effort to agitate or combine against their decisions was treason...

-John A. Armstrong

"Look at the contours of red and orange sandstone formations." I said when we pulled to the first observation point. "Bryce is my favorite canyon. It's not as grandiose as Grand and Zion Canyons, but much more approachable. You can look at these sandstone castles and palaces with their changing contours and shades the whole day long and never get tired. You can pretty easily get all the way down the canyon and look at this beauty from different perspectives. It looks like a myriad of ancient castles and temples on one God given set."

...We spent the rest of the day climbing and sightseeing. We walked from point to point with the most spectacular

54

and at the same time very friendly, even intimate, panoramic views opening in front of our eyes. Myron took close to a thousand pictures with his digital camera. The weather was perfect, sunny, warm and a little breezy, with a few clouds in the sky, giving some special visual effects to the amazing panorama. We settled for lunch at the picnic table, picking some goodies from our cooler, and took a couple of hours break...

"I have talked to you,Myron about Leon Trotsky, the one of the major players in the arena of the communist movement," I went on. *"I think it's important to see how a gifted zealot, obsessed with an asinine idea, can brilliantly execute it, and then helplessly watch it go off the wall."*

"What if you first give me a clearer picture of all of the social movements you are talking about? I don't think they settled well in my mind as a coherent system."

"Well, mine is not the first algorithm used for this classification. See, there are many forms of ideological movements inside of our Western society. The picture isn't exactly black and white, so my algorithm, defining where one belongs, would be simplistic as well. I'll try to develop a questionnaire. You can put your economic and social preferences into this simple formula, and I'll tell you roughly who you are on a political scale, and even who you can potentially become, if you go too far to the extreme. Depending upon your view on the *government interference in solving economic and cultural* issues you can just enter an answer – 'prefer' or 'reject', and you'll find yourself roughly in one of these major categories:

Liberals *prefer* the government economic involvement and *reject* its interference in cultural issues; libertarians *reject* both socio-economic and cultural interference of the state in the life of society; and conservatives *reject* economic interference of the state and *prefer* higher societal involvement in cultural and communal affairs."

"All these political and philosophical movements are healthy and legitimate elements of a free society, aren't they, Deda? They are the source of checks and balances so important for our Republic to function.".

"Yes, Myron. But look at the implications of certain philosophies, if they go to the extreme. The extreme manifestation of liberalism—radical Left—with ideas of total governmental control over economy, taxation, education, healthcare and distribution is pure Socialism and the economic basis for gross abuses of power. The left wing radicals are deluding themselves into thinking that they can preserve their personal freedoms, once socialism is established; but the *government control* over resources and distribution was all Stalin needed to set up his breed of totalitarianism.

The conservatives, however, represent the spirit of solid functional capitalism with free trade and low taxation; but they have to be careful not to fall into a militant breed of religious fundamentalism."

"Or even fascism?"

"No, Myron, this is a common misnomer. True Conservatives are against fascism on just about everything: on sanctity of life, on power of government and taxation, abusive welfare and wealth redistribution, racial relations and aggressive role of minorities. Conservative's disciplinarian approach in cultural issues is often being interpreted as 'Fascism'. To the contrary, Fascism is just another word for Socialism. As you well know, Stalin called his breed of fascism the 'Soviet Socialism'. How did Hitler call his fascism?"

"The National Socialism."

"That's correct, Myron. The word Nazi is just an abbreviation. Fascists are found often on the fringe of a free society.

The moderate libertarian philosophy is my favorite: it's attractive to both liberals and conservatives; and the libertarians have often allied with one or the other of these two movements, but if they go extreme and completely reject any societal control, they are prone to anarchism with its turmoil and lawlessness. Ultimately, when citizens get tired of libertarian chaos, a *strongman* takes total power, with obvious consequences.

As you can see, Myron, every political philosophy, when taken to the extreme, is an open road to totalitarianism. Totalitarianism is a focal point, where all parallel lines of extremism invariably meet somewhere in a convoluted political space. So, to be safe, my dear, just stay away from extremes. Human goodness and love are the only safe extremes. That includes, of course, a genuine love for your Country."

"Agree."

"Any way. Marxists don't want to wait until their socialistic ideas are accepted by the majority. As radicals they are in a tiny minority. Contrary to the bourgeois democratic process, Marxism professes overturning of the existing system by force and establishing the rule of the militant minority, as a jumping board to socialism. The means of getting there is essentially the only difference between Marxism and the modern radical Left; but the *common goal is a communist utopia of the ultimate welfare society with its total state control and complete disconnection from natural human aspirations - pursuance of life, liberty and human happiness.* 'Good socialism' is a delusion leading straight and inescapably to totalitarianism."

"Why is that?"

"Because, Myron, not too many people will work without incentives, unless they are physically forced to do so; and this means good-bye to both democracy and prosperity."

"It seems, Deda, like you are using the terms *socialism, communism and totalitarianism* interchangeably."

"Well... Socialism is an economic structure of society; it determines how society produces and distributes national wealth and who is in charge - the state or an individual. Communism is an ideology of socialism, its ultimate goal: to strip an individual of his civil rights and make him part of a soulless mechanism of the government system. Totalitarianism is an extreme way of oppressive governing, its working tool, the set of such infamous instruments as the secret police, government controlled education, propaganda, and indoctrination. In this sense I use all of them interchangeably—they cover different aspects of the same phenomenon."

"Where would you put yourself on this ideological scale?"

"I guess I'm a traditionalist like an overwhelming majority of moderate Americans. Like many moderates I cherish libertarian values. I am disappointed with corruption and the way both parties in our government are functioning at this point in history to a different extend. I think a limited and efficient government can be selected *by the people and for the people* in this world of high technology. I believe, we should better control the institution of special interest groups, striving for domination of militant minorities over the silent and often complacent majority. Close to my heart are issues like the reckless stand of the radical Left on the tolerance towards the world of evil, its welfare mentality, its political zealotry, and its rejection of boundaries of cultural decency. All of this keeps me in a more traditional camp, somewhat to the right of center."

"Hah, hah... That sounds straight forward."

"Appreciate your sarcasm, my dear."

"Leon Trotsky. I'm trying to figure out why you're so deliberate in describing the predicaments of this character."

" A lot in his story you have to read between the lines. Trotsky was much more ruthless than you think. Some call him a mass murderer. He was exceptionally charismatic. The young generation of his followers adored him like a rock star and just wanted to be him. I'm afraid history never fails to come back on a new level, with new generation of actors and losers, with a complete amnesia about the past."

"I think I know what you mean, Deda. I wonder how much he would have done, if he had put himself to good use, for instance, in charge of a large corporation."

"That's a good thought, Myron. He probably wouldn't care about polls and surely wouldn't rest till the *job's done*. As an Ideologue he knew exactly what he wanted; but in retrospect, with all his talents and determination, he wasted his entire life on a 'hot air balloon'. He was one of the major architects of this monumental disaster. He didn't realize up to the time of his assassination that Stalinism was not a counter-revolution. Stalin's reign of terror was a logical extension and product of a faulty original premise, *the Dictatorship of Proletariat as the first step to Socialism.*"

"So, it looks like the communist idea can't survive without Dictatorship and terror, can it?" Myron wondered, shaking his head.

"It most definitely can't. Its success would be against the common nature of man... Any way, let's see how Leon Trotsky grew up along with the Russian revolutionary environment. The Russian liberal intelligentsia, represented largely by the cultural elite and students, was restless since Pushkin's time, the beginning of the 19th century. It protested against Czarist's oppression, serfdom, poverty, the Russian isolation and backwardness. The Populism stood specifically for the liberation of peasants from an economical noose and governmental oppression. Young Liova Bronstein joined one of these anarchistic terrorist's groups. He didn't assault anyone—he was in charge of writing and the printing of revolutionary proclamations.

In 1897 Leon read Karl Marx's 'Communist Manifesto' and instantly converted himself to a *Social Democrat*. Marxism was a movement with an aim to overturn capitalism by force and establish the first step of a new world order – Socialism. The working class was supposed to be *the avant-garde and ruling class of this revolution*. It should have helped to concentrate all lands and all material means of production in the hands of the state, and distribute 'equitably' the goods between different classes of society. The ultimate long-term goal of this revolution was to be total liquidation of classes and the formation of pure Communism, the rosy paradise on earth, based essentially on a formula as simple as it was profoundly flawed: **From everyone according to his means – to everyone according to his needs."**

"Are you kidding?"

"No, I'm not, Myron. It's a welfare society to its very absurdity; it means centralized education, childcare, healthcare, production and distribution, with the all the means and ways in the hands of government. It's a system with no incentive to contribute and plenty of incentives to consume—unless you are a saint of some kind. It's utopia to an extreme

During all my time, Russia was proclaimed as the Union of Soviet Socialist Republics. A lot of effort was made by the propaganda machine to make an impression that the system was entering a first stage of Communism. All means of production down to shoe-shining businesses had been nationalized. A workers salary was brought to a level so low, that free education, free health care, free childcare and virtually free transportation would come out by default. Raising children from a few months old to adulthood was in the hands of the state—it was really taking a village, a huge bureaucratic village to raise a child; and parents had very little to do with it, since they were busy working and standing in long lines for scarce consumer goods and very basic food staples. Factories and offices were involved in distributing these goods, making the whole system unmanageable and deeply corrupt."

"Why would you need money, Deda, if everything is free? Isn't that Heaven, if I may ask as a devil's advocate?"

"Heaven becomes a Hell when nobody has an incentive to contribute. Society just falls apart, or becomes one huge concentration camp with enforced labor. This *paradise* system, as you'll have plenty of opportunity to learn, was a recipe for economic disaster and the ultimate abuse of power. And (surprise, surprise!) it was just a step ahead of the wildest dreams of our radical Lefties here at home. How would they know that an immensely gifted pinhead like Trotsky, a man of a much higher order of intelligence than our *'brilliant'* leaders, had already landed on his face, trying to build this paradise in Russia, with the intention to impose it on the whole world? Almost a century of a monumental screw-up is not a laughing matter. I had an opportunity to 'enjoy' the full flavor of these massive deadly experiments; and, believe me, it stunk then and won't smell any better now."

"Nobody less than the insane could come out with something like this"

"Many people on the streets in places like New York and San Francisco still believe in this utopia. I have been in heated communication with many of them; and I've given up in despair."

"Perhaps they don't read much, Deda."

"Some don't; but many of them claim to be the best read. Among them are popular Hollywood actors, lawyers, journalists and tenured Professors of major universities."

"Maybe they're just idealists?"

"I couldn't find too many Hollywood stars living by the rules they preach, or giving a good example of conduct."

"Do you find them too vocal?"

"As many radicals, Myron, they always find some

sympathetic welfare-ready audience, particularly among those who can't find their Country on the map. Remember Tyler's statement that the decline of democracy starts with the voter, who prefers the giver to a doer as his leader."

"I listened to their arguments, Deda. I think there is a lot of unfairness in this world, and they may be right to go after them."

"I'm glad you wonder; but I don't think you would even like what these Hollywood Zombies preach... In any case, Myron, let me continue, if you want to take a look behind the kitchen door of this revolution just a bit."

"OK. Just a little bit."

"The 'Classic' Marxism, originated in Central Europe, targeted well-developed capitalism. The backward country, which was just out of serfdom, with the medieval oppression, embryonic working class, and the overwhelming majority of its citizens working the soil and shoveling the cow and horse manure, Russia, according to Karl Marx, wasn't ready yet...Not to Lenin, though."

"Tell me about him."

"Well, let's see...Imagine a man with the body of a pygmy, brain of Socrates, the ambition and drive of Napoleon, the captivating orator with a funny whirr, the figure you wouldn't otherwise notice on the street. He had come out with an idea—people of this stature often need a white horse or a big stamp to be visible. He developed his *Russian* version of Marxism, *'The Leninism'*. According to his theory, there is no better place in the world for socialism and communism than a country, where the most sophisticated tilling machine was a mattock, and 95 percent of the population doesn't know how to read. 'So what?' he said. 'Cleaner the sheet - easier to write on it. At least they know how to raise the hands'."

"Exactly in those words?"

"Close… So, the driving force of a socialist revolution was supposed to be the Social Democratic Labor Party— renamed later as a *Communist Party of the Soviet Union.* The central organ of the Party, during the preparation of the revolution, would be a small group of disciplined, professional and highly conspiratorial revolutionaries in exile. The Party would eventually have an overwhelming power, over any other state institution. Lenin from the very beginning planned the authoritarian rule of a 'good leader', a concept that quickly proved to be a prescription for the abuse of power, cult of personality, and ultimately – totalitarianism. In his polemics and argumentation Lenin used quotations from the thinkers like Marx, Engels, Hegel etc, and presented them as absolute authorities—he didn't need any historical proof of failure or success. He utilized his unquestionable genius as a debater and 'nice guy', and spun the facts any way he wanted. In turn, the Soviet authorities, the followers of Leninism, including Stalin, quoted Lenin in the same manner, all the time out of context, to justify every move in their policies."

"Just like that? Doesn't that sound a bit similar to nowadays rhetoric?"

"That's right, young man. Demagogues make their statements axiomatic, no scientific proof is required."

"So, Lenin was like founder and chairman of the board of this giant 'corporation' called Russia."

"You can say that."

"Tell me, Deda, how could a small group of exiles conduct revolutionary activity in such a huge and complex country like Russia?"

"Well; let's talk about that when we are back to the hotel. We still have some climbing to do. The highest observation point in the area, *The Inspiration Point*, is yet to be conquered. What if you, young man, run quickly to our original parking and bring our car closer. I'll start slowly ascending toward our summit in the mean time. I call this the Senior Privilege..."

We reached *Inspiration Point* at the right time of the day. The incredible view of the Canyon amphitheater with the hoodoos, vertical cliffs and the green valley outlined by the mountain ranges behind, had opened in front and below. The sun descended to a position of shading every individual eroded crevice. Occasional clouds shaded certain portions of the landscape, moving these shades along the intricate slopes, making them look alive. We took countless pictures and videos of this fascinating live display of nature in its process. It was a humbling experience. The most beautiful spirit of Deity surely resides in this place!

*****

We came to our room exhausted, hungry and sunburned. After dinner we settled in the cozy hotel lobby, and I followed up:

"Do you really want to hear how they cooked up this revolution?" I asked Myron carefully.

"Of course, Deda. They created a major upheaval of the century in the name of *change*, and I would like to learn more about how it came about, and how to prevent it from happening to us in any form.I want to hear your opinion."

"Unlike many *Progressives* you are progressing with an impressive speed, Young Man... Well, the coming revolution had its trumpet, an underground periodic publication called *Iskra* (the Spark). It was edited and printed in Zurich, Switzerland, in the form of a small newspaper, and delivered to Russia via a long route, normally through the Balkans, Turkey and Caucasus. The editorial Board consisted originally of six professional revolutionaries, residing in Zurich. The editors would digest sporadic information from home, which would come by messengers or in coded mail, and then they composed the news articles, political analysis and directives. In essence, the Iskra Board was the brain center of the movement, a bunch of orators with no idea how convert theory into practice of bread baking.

When 23-year old Trotsky escaped from Siberian exile in 1902 to Zurich, he was, at Lenin's insistence, hired as an editor and writer in the Iskra's staff. He switched between different factions of Iskra a few times, and then *landed solidly with Lenin.*"

"In the mean time," I continued my story, "the events in Russia developed pretty much independently from the conspiratorial activity of Iskra. Russia admitted its defeat in the war with Japan, when the Russian Pacific fleet was demolished at Tsusima, on the far East. Ignited by the war, the Russian industrial revolution took off rapidly, particularly in Moscow and St. Petersburg, the centers of working class concentration. Strikes and demonstrations for an improvement of working and living conditions erupted. The priest Gapon, the popular political figure among Russian orthodox masses, organized one of these demonstrations. It was a peaceful demonstration. On Sunday morning of January 9, 1905 over two hundred thousand workers, with wives and children, started their march toward the Czar's palace in St. Petersburg. They carried a petition and placards, pleading for their *Father-Czar* to straighten out the corrupt and abusive government officials. Police and the emperor's guards opened fire. Over 500 men, women and children were killed, 3000 – wounded. The *Bloody Sunday* went into the annals of history and ignited the first Russian revolution.

In October the general strike paralyzed the Russian economy. The Czar came out with a Manifesto, which allowed the formation of Duma, the first elected figurehead institution in Russian history, and also pledged to tolerate some political associations. This 'democracy' was then quickly reversed; the the leaders of a newly formed St. Petersburg's Soviet of Workers Representatives were arrested, and a few of them, including Trotsky, were sent to Siberian exile. This was Trotsky's second exile, from which he again escaped to the West.

To flee completely isolated, extremely inhospitable, and heavily guarded areas thousands of miles away from any civilization was a monumental and dangerous task. On his first escape, Trotsky had to leave his wife and two daughters behind and practically lost his first family. As you can see, the change—good or bad—comes around not easy... Now, if you wish, I can tell you about Trotsky's idea of *Permanent Revolution*."

"I'm falling asleep. Let's continue tomorrow morning. Okay, Deda?"

"I'm tired too; let me finish with this topic, it won't take long."

"You've got five minutes of my attention."

"Deal! ...As I said before, the Mensheviks who were abiding by the teachings of Classic Marxism, suggested of using Parliament (Duma) as an instrument of a bloodless transition to capitalism, and then push to socialism and communism. Lenin, however, relied on a small group of elite, highly disciplined revolutionary intelligentsia, to lead masses directly from weakened Czarism to socialism, skipping capitalism altogether. The goal of Trotsky's Permanent Revolution would than be to support socialist revolutions all over the world to justify its name – *Permanent*. Lenin often shifted his own equation in favor of the idea of Permanent Revolution. As you would learn, the February of 1917 Bourgeois revolution, which quickly followed by the Bolshevik's October putsch, was the brainchild of these two *intellectual machines*."

"So, this is how we all got screwed over for seventy years,

is it?"

"You have it right again. This is how we got screwed over indeed; and not just for seventy years."

5

Winning by Default

"War between Austria and Russia would be a very useful thing for the revolution, but it's not likely that Franz Joseph and Nikolashka will give us this pleasure."

-Lenin in 1913

"*Nikolashka* (the czar Nicholas II) has certainly provided Bolsheviks with this opportunity," I continued yesterday's subject, when we checked out of our hotel and embraced scenic Route 89 on our way to Lake Powell. "Look at cynicism--the 'fighter for the Russian peoples paradise' wouldn't hesitate a minute to start a world war and sacrifice millions of lives just to help his ambitious plans. Any price was just right to him for the power grab. Than after the the putsch Lenin instantly converted himself into a 'Peacenik'.

"Nice flip! How did Lenin use this war, Deda? Did he just wait for the warring sides to exhaust themselves?"

"Not at all, Myron. When WWI started in 1914 with a terrorist act in Sarajevo, Lenin got busy demoralizing the Russian army. He sent hundreds of agitators against an *imperialistic* war, promising 'bread to workers and land to peasants', and persuaded them to desert the front lines.

The revolution started with demonstrations and then riots in Petrograd[1]. Slogans were: 'End to the war! End to autocracy'. Some loyal troops switched sides. Liberal democrats and social-revolutionaries took control, formed a provisional government of the first Russian Bourgeois Democratic Republic and forced the Czar to abdicate. The Russian monarchy had become history, replaced with social democracy."

"The Bolsheviks, in the mean time," I went on, "formed their legislative and executive governing body – the Petrograd Soviet[2], which became a school of the Bolshevik Revolution with a Dictatorship of Proletariat as a goal. Two competing powers took hold. Bolsheviks were gaining confidence. The Lenin's flip had worked."

---

[1] Revolutionary version of St. Petersburg

[2] Workers Council

"Was it something like the two major parties in an American Congress," Myron mused.

"Not quite, Myron. They were two separate governments with diametrically opposing agendas. On the Republic's side it was a multi-party democratic system trying to establish constitutional rule of law. The Bolsheviks, being originally in minority, were not interested in real democracy. Lenin and Trotsky used a mockery of democratic process in the Petrograd Soviet to promote a Dictatorship of Proletariat, that later deteriorated into full blown totalitarianism. In his Biography Leon Trotsky, on a personal example, very eloquently described how the Dictatorship of Proletariat, this 'innocent' brainchild of his mind, had functioned.

Trotsky, his wife, his two boys and a housekeeper lived in an apartment located in a Petrogtad's relatively up-scaled community. They found themselves surrounded by the bourgeoisie and middle class people, who didn't have much respect for the 'pushy Reds'. Trotsky wrote:

> The situation was growing more and more antagonistic. But one fine day the house blockade ceased as abruptly as if somebody had lifted it with an all-powerful hand. When the head janitor met my wife he would make a bow such as only the most important tenants were privileged to receive.

At the House committee, the bread was issued without delays or threats. No one banged doors in our faces now. Who had achieved this change—what magician? It was Nikolay Markin. I must give an account of him, because through him, or rather through a collective Markin, the October revolution was victorious.

Markin was a sailor in the Baltic navy. He was illiterate, shy, sullen, and cut all as one piece. He conveyed an impression of a person one can't cross. He established the Dictatorship of Proletariat in Trotsky's house even before the Bolshevik Revolution. He would come not alone, but with a group of sailors, and use very persuasive words to establish 'piece and fairness'.

After the Bolshevik revolution Markin became indispensible as a Trotsky's silent but powerful guard and assistant. One day, with the revolver in his hands, he was fighting for a 'sober October', guarding the wine stores. When it was impossible to stop a looting mob, he would destroy the stock. 'In high boots, buried in a broken glass, soaked to the skin and exuding the fragrance of the choicest wines', he was a symbol of the Proletarian revolution. The next day, he was on another front: answering a phone in Trotsky's office of the Commissar of Foreign Affairs."

"What a character, Deda. Were there many characters like this among the Bolsheviks!"

"More than you can imagine; they were hungry for power and action. The reason I told you this story is to show how difficult it is sometimes to separate the good intentions and character from political and philosophical delusions that result in a horrendous outcome. Think, Myron, beyond the emotional value of Trotsky's story. You can see how appealing the idea of socialism can be. In the hands of a 'good leader', by Lenin's definition, it can move mountains. The fruits of this malignant idea are shown through the whole history of Bolshevism."

"Tell me, Deda, in short, how the Bolshevik revolution proceeded? Was it tough fight?"

"Well; the future bloodiest regime in the history of the human race *bloodlessly* came to power in October 25, 1917. Lenin and Trotsky spent a sleepless night after they sent Red Guards and Sailors to storm the Winter Palace, where the Provisional Government of the Republic was barricaded with some cadets of the Military Academy. The army had deserted them, when Bolsheviks successfully exploited this war and now were firmly against it. The cruiser Aurora shot a symbolic round, which harmlessly landed on the Palace plaza, and the defenders surrendered. The government was waiting in one room for their fate...

Later in school we were fed numerous stories and saw the wall-to-wall paintings about the bloody battle for the Winter Palace. But amazingly, none of the priceless relics of the Palace's monumental museums were broken—so much for the *bloody battle*. Appropriately enough, the cruiser Aurora was for 70 years the most precious museum item and the symbol of the revolution. The easy part was accomplished. The challenge of a morning hangover had just begun.

The relatively painless take-over was followed by a bloody Civil War. The new Soviet (Red) army had to be created. Trotsky became a Commissar (Minister) of the war. It started with a rebellion of Czecho-Slovak regimen of the war prisoners on Volga River. For starters, the newborn army had to fight the foreign invasion, the White Guards[1] (troops of overthrown Provisionary Government); and Cossacks[2] The bands of Anarchists, Nationalists, and simply terrorists were roaming around creating havoc. Everybody—at the same time or in sequence—rose against this revolution."

"How much territory had the Bolsheviks retained at the worst point, Deda?"

---

[1] Officers of a Czarist army.

[2] Troops of free military settlements formed to defend frontiers, *russ.*

78

"About fifteen to twenty percent, as I remember."

"Holy Molly! And Trotsky had to handle that?"

"He was running around like a maniac in his armored train from one front to another, where the situation hung beyond salvation. In his words he 'made around this globe several times'. His 'best' invention was the double front line, with a second one behind the fighting front line. The second line contained party members, the guards, with an order to shoot any one who retreated from his position. It took five bloody years before Bolsheviks came out victorious and restored Russian territory almost to the original size of the Empire. Stalin, by the way, used Trotsky's invention during WWII very extensively—the commissars even encouraged the Soviet Army soldiers to use their bodies as *plugs* for the Nazi bunker's embrasures."

"I had no idea about the scope of Trotsky's effort."

"Naturally. When he was Stalin's exile, nobody in the West cared to remember him. For us in Russia, the word 'Trotskyism' was one of the dirtiest in the vocabulary. What could we behind the Iron Curtain know about this radical Left zealot, condemned by his own party. Stalinism was very skillful in rewriting history."

"Bolsheviks had to deal with a monumental mess they created, didn't they?"

"Indeed, they had. Russia was in ruin and starvation when

Lenin declared a State of Emergency and *Martial Law Communism*, which meant: every producer of an agricultural product could keep for himself only enough to barely survive and give up the rest to the state. This measure was quickly abolished, when peasants preferred to fight or burn their grain, rather than give it to the government officials."

"So much for the first experience with communism!"

"Right. Finally, Lenin, this smart politician, came out with the idea of a NEP, the 'New Economic Policy"—nothing less than capitalism within socialism. Until his death in January 1924 he watched with dismay how successfully this healthy, vigorous and often wild capitalism was ravaging his idea of communism. Do you remember, Myron, when you visited your Grandmother in Russia, before the Country started to show some signs of stability. You, Myron, know how vigorous the new capitalism have become after the disintegration of the Soviet Union?"

"Yes I do... So, Bolsheviks created the mess they almost buried themselves in, didn't they?"

"Well, there is a diabolical rule which the radical minority of zealots always employs with a good deal of success: *Bring your Country down to a chaos, grab power with bare hands, and blame your opponents for all the sufferings of the innocents.*"

"You are alluding to our current situation, aren't you? It looks like we lost any hope in the future positive developments. This is not what our Country has always been all about."

"I'm glad you found my parallels not too much of a stretch... Any way, the October Revolution and the following Civil War had ended the initial period of idealism and illusion in the communist movement. Time came for reality—the isolation from the world and a complete incarceration of almost half a billion people behind the Iron Curtain. This was the inevitable result of the liberal utopia...But it's time for bed, Baby. Tomorrow, after the tour around Lake Powell, we will get a little *personal*."

"What do you mean?"

"You'll see, Myron, someone I loved and admired, was in the middle of this turmoil."

*****

"You promised to get personal. I'm intrigued," Myron insisted, when we were comfortably situated in the hotel lobby after lunch, following our beautiful boat tour around Lake Powell.

"Well, believe it or not, your paternal great grandfather's

family was at the center of some civil war events in Ukraine. They lived then on the outskirt of a little Jewish ghetto-town Kazatin in the central Ukraine district of Zhitomir. My father's grandfather Haim Khmelinsky rented a parcel of land from the landowner—the army officer living in Kiev—and tended his little farm. He was the local milkman. On the faded century old photo he even looked pretty much like *Tev'eh the Milkman,* played by Topol in the famous Broadway musical *Fiddler on the Roof.* When Haim passed away, his older son Isaiah, my grandfather, took over the family 'operation'. When Czar Alexander II removed the Jewish privileges to buy or rent the land, Isaiah somehow managed to remain an employee of the landlord, tending his horses. The farmhouse they lived in was a tiny dwelling with an attached hayloft. In the middle of the yard there was a deep well with a bucket on a long rope and a crank-drum. At the time of this revolution, the family had two cows, a horse, and a few goats with a bunch of chickens running around. A little vegetable garden also helped to sustain their life. By local standards of the ghetto of Jewish settlement Isaiah was doing relatively well. The family wasn't overly orthodox, but diligently attended all Holidays in the local prayer house.

My father, Efraim, nine at the beginning of the civil war,

was the youngest one in the family, with two sisters – Clara and Hannah, and three brothers – Yakov, Lev and the oldest Elia. Lev and Elia were married, and Elia lived separately in Kazatin, working as a blacksmith—he was active in the local Jewish Worker's Union. The rest of the family worked on the farm and inhabited the tight quarters there. Yakov, nineteen, had a dream to become a veterinarian. He loved to deal with animals, was literate in Ukrainian and Russian, but didn't have enough formal educational opportunity in the little town of Kazatin. My grandmother Esther, of course, was a ruling force in the family, just like in any Jewish *patriarchal* household. Everybody in the family was strong, handsome, over six feet tall, except my father and his sister Hannah, seventeen. Both were tiny, inseparable, and everyone called them "Cuddly Ducklings". My father attended a local one-room Hebrew school, and Hannah helped in milking and selling some produce on the local market. She was a strikingly beautiful girl with thick braids around her head and huge brown eyes. I just gave you a little synopsis for your future genealogical research, Myron, if you ever get interested in one."

"Sounds idyllic, almost biblical. It's so good to know all this stuff."

"They were a tight family doing okay, but the outside

world was different. My father told me about his childhood only after WWII, when I was about sixteen. When he mentioned Hannah and Yakov, his lips trembled and his eyes filled with tears. 'We never talked about Hannah and Yakov in mother's presence', he said. 'We lost them tragically during the civil war, and in both cases we almost lost our mother, so difficult it was for her'."

"Tell me please about that."

"Hannah was in love with Ben, the Hebrew-school teacher, a quiet scholarly young man. Everything was arranged for them to get married. Life, however, had its own plans. The year of 1918 was a beginning of the bloodiest pogroms (anti-Semitic riots) in the history of Jewish ghettoes in Ukraine. The bands of thugs were so numerous - nobody knew when the ambush was going to occur; and when they did, they tortured, plundered, burned and murdered. The counter-revolutionary propaganda against Jews—who were held by many as a major force of a liberal movement against the Czarist's absolutism—ran wild, and the fascist groups, like the infamous Black Hundred, originated and were encouraged all over the country.

One day Hannah stopped by the school in the middle of the session after her market day. She sat next to my father, just to watch the teaching process and be in one room with

Ben for a moment, and then to drive their buggy home with her little brother. The band of thugs ambushed the school. They bludgeoned Ben to death in front of the pupils, torched the school, grabbed Hannah, threw her in the buggy, and ran away with her. She was never seen again. There were rumors that it was the work of a local Ukrainian, who stalked Hannah often, when she was at the market, and then disappeared to join a band of terrorists."

"And your father never told you about that, when you were a kid?"

"He was probably afraid to traumatize me, or show his emotions—fathers don't cry in front of little kids. But he had never gotten over that horror. He sobbed, when I asked him to tell me more about his sister."

"I read about your father in your book. He was your icon in the pre-war time. Then he went to WWII, fought the entire war as a foot soldier, was decorated, and came back to struggle to keep the family afloat. Was he any different after the war?"

"We all were very different after that horrendous experience; and I was a teenager, with my life to handle. My father was there for us, always everybody's friend. But he was not a happy man any more. I guess he came home with a Post-Traumatic Stress Syndrome. Some people in this condition were drinking and lashing out. Not my father! He quietly withdrew inside himself. Probably as a result he suffered from stomach ulcers and respiratory problems."

"Too bad I never knew him, Deda."

"Yes, unfortunately he passed away two years before you were born. I wasn't there with him when he died so suddenly."

"So--coming back to a Civil War time--how did your father's family survive all this turmoil?"

"Troubles were just approaching their peak. In November 1918 Ukraine declared independence. Symon Petlura, the co-founder of the Ukrainian Labor Party, a staunch Ukrainian Nationalist, and an officer of the Czar's army in the times between revolutions of 1905 and 1917—a 'nice' and not uncommon combination—became the governing head and Minister of War in a new government. Petlura instigated, or at least turned his blind eye to the campaign of genocide against Jews. In Ukraine alone 50,000 Jews were killed in the period 1919-20, with majority murdered by Petlura's forces.

Jews, where it was possible, formed neighborhood groups of resistance. One of the resistance centers was on my father's farm. Elia had gotten a "Maxim" machine gun somewhere and fixed it. The Maxim was an automatic gun on two wheels and with a big steel shield. It was the most popular weapon of the Civil War. It could be put on a horse cart or buggy, making it a very mobile fortress, called *'Tachanka'*. The ancient chariot served probably as a prototype of this powerful weapon. Some neighbors joined with he and his wife Maya at the farm house. They managed to repel a few vicious attacks. In one of these skirmishes Yakov was killed. His Hebrew name was Israel. In his memory I carry the same Hebrew name."

"You never told me how you got your name, Deda."

"Now you know; and I can see why it was so difficult for my father to talk about that...

In the mean time, in 1923, the Red Army moved against combined forces of Poles and Petlura and pushed them out of Ukraine. Then fortune got shaky again, Petlura showed signs of revival, and my father's family didn't want to take any chances. They moved with the retreating Red Army to a cold and hungry Moscow, where they had some friends. That's where my father and mother met, and where I was born in 1933, a year ravaged by famine, and brought upon Russia by Stalin's agricultural collectivization—you've read about that in the first book.

Petlura didn't escape his moment of ultimate justice. On May 25, 1926, while shopping along the boulevard in Paris, he was approached by the man, who asked him in Ukrainian: 'Are you Mister Petlura?' After receiving affirmation, the man, Ukrainian born Jewish anarchist, Sholom Schwarzbard, pulled out a gun shooting Petlura three times, shouting: 'This is for the pogroms; this is for the massacres; this is for the victims.' Sholom's parents were among fifteen members of his family, murdered in the pogroms... A French jury acquitted him."

"It's a very sad story, Deda."

"It is, Myron... Do you know how late it is, young man? Tomorrow is another day.

6

From Fantasy to Reality

The 'Informer' system became Stalin's practical instrument for destroying his adversaries and consolidating his own position. And for his subordinates, informing was a way to prove their loyalty, to gain their leader's favor.

—Yuri Druzhnikov, Russian journalist and political scientist.

"You have been talking about Lenin and Trotsky as major architects of this revolution" Myron begun when we took off from Page towards the Southern Rim of the Grand Canyon, following the scenic Route 89 South. "You never mentioned Stalin, as if Stalinism was separate phenomenon. Where was Stalin during the Bolshevik revolution?"

"Stalin was the optimal figure in materializing all the

genetic traits of the system. At the beginning of the Soviet rule he wasn't there much at all. He robbed the banks to provide cash for the movement, and engaged in some small-scale activities. He was even arrested and sent to Siberia, from where he escaped. This, by the way, he made a key point in his resume. His very insignificance, ironically, was his best protection and striking tool, when he accused his active and quite prominent opponents of mistakes and flaws, for nobody is immune from blunders. He became really busy, though, after the Bolshevik Revolution."

"How did it happen? Why him?"

"Let's, Myron, go briefly through his life—Stalin's background is quite relevant for understanding his motives and methods:

Joseph (Soso) Djugashvili-Stalin was born December 1878 in Gori, a small town in the central mountainous region of the Kingdom of Georgia, on the southern outskirts of European Russia. Two thousand years before Muscovy came to the world stage, this region was a mountain pass of ancient civilizations, with some peaks among the highest in Europe: The 'Mount Ararat' (17,000 feet high) was the legendary place of landing of Noah's Ark; and the 'Kasbek' (16,500 feet) - the mountain, on which Greek's Super God Zeus chained the mythological revolutionist

Prometheus. On the summit of 'Elbrus' (18,500 feet above sea level) the gigantic stature of Joseph Stalin was later erected with the legend on it seen far away: 'On the highest crest of Europe we have erected the bust of the greatest man of our time'."

"Sounds like it's a beautiful area, Deda. Have you been there?"

"Yes, it's a gorgeous area, the only place for downhill skiing in the former USSR, an entertainment that was affordable only to the Bolshevik's elite and black marketers. It was also a prosperous area. From Egypt and Mesopotamia the smelting and forging of metals spread to Armenia and Georgia, while the Eurasian plane lived for many centuries more in the Stone Age. Two of the oldest Christian kingdoms in the world, Armenia and Georgia, were converted to Orthodox Christianity more than half a millennium before the Kievan Russia threw away their idols."

"What happened to all this rich culture and history, Deda?"

"A tiny bit of it is still there. But if Georgia entered earlier into history, it also left it earlier, as happened with many ancient civilizations. In this respect I am worrying about our Western civilization. Some serious studies of historical trends find a lot of similarities between Western civilization and the Roman Empire before she fell to the

Barbarians—the same disregard of values, the same apathy and complacency. Just think about it, Myron. What can we do in the West to prevent this common cycle from entering the reality of our Republic? Are we destined to succumb to a new barbarianism as well? What should we do about it? I refuse to accept it as something inevitable."

"I guess, we in the West tend to think about our way of life as something given, without much of an appreciation of its advantages. This syndrome bothers me too, Deda. It sucks, but that's how people are!"

"I'm happy you are thinking that way—it's your world now... So, back to Georgia. From the late Middle Ages up to the automobile era with its oil demand, this mountainous land hibernated. Trapped for centuries between the hammer of the Turks and the anvil of the Persians, it finally asked for Russian protection. Russia changed the request to a *conquest*, detached the whole region from Asia and incorporated it into Europe. Yet, this old connection with Turkey and Iran was to deeply influence the Russian foreign policy and overall character and philosophy of the future Russian ruler, Joseph Stalin. Unlike Lenin, *Stalin never rid himself of a strong emotional attachment to the culture and attitude of isolation, intolerance and vendetta, associated too often with this neighboring region down South.* His background was a seminary, which he abandoned for a revolutionary activity. This hardly left him much opportunity to get in touch with goodness of Lev Tolstoy, Shakespeare or Avicenna."

"Background of a street-smart gangster?"

"Yes. He was the street-smart Mafioso, and the bazaar environment was his school of life... Georgia was populated with so many rival ethnic groups, that the Bolsheviks had to divide it into seventeen *Autonomous* regions and republics. On top of that, lots of migrants settled in the area. So, in his childhood Soso Djugashvili, in addition to local natives, rubbed shoulders with Turks, Tartars, Persians, Greeks, Kurds, Jews, Moldavians, Estonians, Czechs, Poles, and of course, the Ukrainians and Great (native) Russians. He had never learned any of those languages though, and spoke a quite limited Russian with a heavy Georgian accent all his life."

"You still have your accent, Deda."

"Thank you, dear! Some are advising me to keep it that way. When I call a stranger second time I don't have to reintroduce myself; it's convenient... In any case; upon the Bolshevik revolution, one of Stalin's appointments in the new government was a Commissar of National Affairs— the regime had to deal with more than a hundred ethnic minorities in this vast country of the Soviet Union, and

Stalin seemed to be a logical candidate, although Lenin and Trotsky were always very leery of him.

This position gave Stalin a perfect trampoline to his next step to absolute power. In a political system with the highly disciplined party as the only deciding institution in the state, with no checks and balances in sight, his coveted target was the post of General Secretary of the Party Central Committee. From this position he would then make a final leap to the position of Chairman, which Lenin occupied until he passed away. Lenin had looked for the 'perfect leader' in his utopian system. The regime started with idealistic utopia and ended up with an utmost ruthless ruler, tyrant and assassin. This is a common paradox of the System"

"I learned, Deda, that he killed just in his purges and 'de-privatization' process more than 30 million Soviet citizens, in which only a tiny part were his real opponents. What was the purpose? Wasn't it just a self-defeating madness?"

"He was a pathological narcissist and terrorist. His strategy and way of thinking in dealing with his opponents, as I mentioned before, was to kill the whole clan, including babies—it's safer this way. In fact, he was, to a large extent, the role model for all successive totalitarian rulers of Nazi Germany, communist China, North Korea, Cuba, and also of the modern Islamic extremist leaders. He spent a couple of years in his position of Commissar of National Affairs quite productively, building a coalition of friends and supporters among different ethnic groups and within the state bureaucratic apparatus. He wouldn't snub any 'useful' method: lie, slander, deceit, blackmail, and assassination. He was busy like a spider and patient like a cobra. I've already mentioned to you that Lenin was preparing Trotsky as his successor. When Lenin got ill and then died, Stalin put his coalition to work and got elected Chairman of the party's Politburo[1], He kept this post until he died in March of 1953."

"So, Stalin invented a quite effective system, considering his rapid rise, didn't he?"

"I don't think he invented it. He was a ruthless executioner of the government power that is naturally coming with Socialism. In fact, it was Lenin who developed the concept of the so-called 'highly disciplined' party apparatus. Modern socialists in turn are learning a lot from the monsters of history."

*****

We were now at the Yavapai Observation Station of the

---

[1]Ruling hub of the Communist Party, *russ*

Grand Canyon Park, on its Southern Rim. We didn't want to miss this time of day to see the spectacular view along the Canyon, before the sun got too low to blind us. Then we proceeded along the rim towards the Village, making some observation stops. We still had time for a late lunch and to find a nice point to see the Grand Canyon sunset. We followed West along the rim and found a comfortable spot at the Hopi Point. The Northern rim had just started to break its shades and colors.

We settled on the ledge of the rim for the upcoming sunset and continued our conversation...

"So, Stalin knew how to play the System created for him by Lenin and Trotsky. How did he proceed?" Myron mused.

"He proceeded with Machiavellian proficiency. There was a bunch of *Old Bolsheviks*, the originators of the October Revolution around. They were in the key positions of the party, in the legislative branch (Soviets) and the executive branch (Commissariats). They had to be pushed out— some of them were 'too noisy'. Thinking about physical elimination, however, was too early and risky at this point. Stalin kept posture of a cobra.

As a first tactical step, Stalin offered a radical policy toward 'Socialism in a Single Country'. This meant turning to a defensive posture, isolating Russia from the world, and pushing for the *Five Year Plan* of building the state controlled industry and collective agriculture. The masses, tired of war and hunger, conceded to abandon Trotsky's drive toward the *worldwide Permanent Revolution.* Stalin's henchmen inflated the occasional Trotsky's academic disagreements with Lenin's theory as a major condemning argument against him. The Trotskyites were pushed off their positions one by one, put on trial, and many of them jailed. Trotsky was too big and too popular a hero of *Red October* to be jailed. He was relieved of his post of the *Commissary of War*, isolated, and left alone for awhile. As I said before, Trotsky called Stalin's campaign the Counter-revolution. But this was a logical continuation of the idea of the Bolshevik Revolution."

"Why, Deda, had Stalin chosen isolation from the outside world? This was not a very 'Marxist' move."

"Here we come again to a funny paradox of the System. Stalin wasn't a Marxist, he was fascist. He used the popular communist slogans to establish totalitarianism. The idealistic Old Bolsheviks of the October revolution became redundant and the objects of his private ridicule. They had done their job, they established the dictatorship and had to get now out of the way. The liberal intellectual elite of revolutionary leadership was now replaced by a more agreeable, more arrogant and ruthless gang of supporters.

Stalin had his plan. He was Middle-Asian in his background, but he also adapted a great deal of Mongolian mentality. When in the 13th century Russia was invaded by the Mongolian hordes, Khan Batu, the supreme ruler of his vast empire, came out with a brilliant idea of *bureaucracy* to keep the empire intact. He would set local authorities or use local warlords in the conquered territories, giving them some autonomy, as long as they collected the required taxes and supported him. As a payment for absolute loyalty Khan would let them do with their subjects whatever they wished. Czarism adapted this system and ruled its empire using this tool for almost seven hundred years. Stalin, in turn, perfected it under the umbrella of 'Leninism' and, as you will see, used methods of the most ruthless Russian rulers like *Ivan the Terrible, Peter the Great* and others."

"So, he apparently did have a perfectly loyal instrument at his disposal, didn't he?"

"Exactly, Myron—he was dedicated, vicious and relentless in his intimidation, slander and indoctrination. He used Old Bolsheviks Kamenev and Zinoviev to denounce Trotsky. His next move was to finish with Trotsky by exiling him to the China frontier for a year, and than deporting him to Turkey as I had already mentioned. In the mean time he eliminated Zinoviev and Kamenev, who already had served their role as renegades. When they showed signs of disappointment with Stalin's policies, they were promptly executed. Stalin's high level helpers for this task were Bukharin and Rykov, the right wings of the Party. They were *neutralized* in turn, when their views became 'too radical'. The list can go on and on. Stalin's manipulation of his friends and enemies was growing in proficiency; the propaganda and indoctrination of masses became more and more professional—Stalin was in the process of building the most efficient propaganda machine in the history of mankind. The Russian population was buying Stalin's explanations of any event with no questions asked. Who would challenge the *'Messiah'* without suffering broken legs or worse? This was the way people felt living in this environment in the Soviet Union. It was terrible and dark time of oppression.

Up to 1934, none of the arrested Old Bolsheviks had been executed. This taboo was broken soon enough, when in December of that year Sergey Kirov, a charismatic politician, the right hand and possible Stalin's successor and even competitor was assassinated. The majority of the previously prosecuted Old Bolsheviks were immediately rearrested, accused in a plot to kill Stalin and other leaders, and executed, in most cases along with their entire families. Many historians suggested later that this Kirov's assassination thing was the clever way for Stalin to kill two birds in one shot—to get rid of the popular competitor and *annoying* Old Bolsheviks.

This was, Myron, the beginning of the infamous *Stalin's political purges.* They lasted 20 years until Stalin's demise. The genocide had rid Russia of the cream of the crop of society; among them: engineers, scientists, generals, medical doctors, artists, writers, etc, whoever could raise a voice. The whole country in the eyes of the maniac and of an indoctrinated public was filled with 'saboteurs'. And the checks and balances were nowhere in sight. It was a self-feeding and self-defeating frenzy."

"You mentioned that Lenin was aware of the terrible pitfalls of the system he created. Why, Deda, couldn't he and Trotsky isolate or simply get rid of Stalin. He wasn't too much of a figure at the beginning of the movement, was he?"

"The irony of Socialism under Dictatorship of Proletariat is that once it starts rolling, it obtains a life of its own. Paradoxically, it was Lenin who appointed Stalin the head of the *Inspection Commission*, collecting compromising information about State employees. Stalin used OGPU, the Secret Police apparatus, to collect compromising information—both genuine and concocted—about people of his personal interest, long before this appointment. The *informer system* became a powerful instrument for destroying his opponents and consolidating his position. As I remember my time in Russia, Myron, we were always afraid to talk to anyone about anything that could be interpreted in a compromising way. We suspected every *dvornik*[1] or repairman to be an informant. For Stalin's immediate subordinates, informing was a way to show their loyalty and gain favor. For the thoroughly indoctrinated dvornik it was his way to 'serve' the country and feel an important part of the system. Some participated enthusiastically and often slandered people they didn't like and wished to get rid of. Everyone spied on everyone, and almost always, the accused would be found guilty before he could even open his mouth to defend himself—*just to make sure that no real enemy would slip through the cracks.*

Under his leadership Stalin formed a *State Complaint Bureau* for collecting the denunciations. He essentially created a massive library of possible and imaginable offences, to be used by the prosecutors and OGPU, when they fabricated cases against innocent victims—it isn't

---

[1] Street sweeper, *russ*

easy, you know, to convict millions of innocents and not look bad without such a 'data base'. That was the best of Stalin's ingenuity."

"It's horrible, Deda. It looks like a deliberate corruption of the very soul of an entire country on a massive scale. I would make this SOB go through all the pain he caused."

"It just shows quite vividly, that *when socio-political system is fundamentally dysfunctional, the totalitarian oppression is the only tool of keeping it from falling apart.*"

"Iron fist vs. freedom?"

"Yes, and that's not all, Myron. The Soviet press was a de facto under complete control of the Complaint Bureau. The denunciation became an everyday function of the press. A newspaper's condemnation was as powerful as the court's sentence. Children were also actively involved in the process. Lenin's widow Nadezhda Krupskaya was at some point in charge of education as a deputy of the People's Commissar of Cultural Affairs. She persuaded little children 'to be observant and to help the Party in eradicating state enemies'. Hundreds of the most enthusiastic little informers were praised in the press and rewarded with a few weeks in *Artek*, the most prestigious Young Lenin Pioneers' camp on the Black Sea, the twisted communist version of the American top-notch innocent

Boy and Girl Scout camps... I see you shivering in disgust, Myron. I just wanted to lead you gently to a realization that totalitarianism in any form always uses the same methods; and that we have to recognize and reject even its embryo in the world around us."

"I don't mean to get 'cute', Deda. But isn't this what we are trying to do to Muslim-Americans now by profiling and wire tapping them, or penetrating their society with informers?"

"It's not being *cute*--it's an excellent question, Myron. It is haunting us to the point of hysteria, as it's supposed to be with decent people. Let me draw parallels with Stalinism and radical Islam. If I am convincing enough, maybe I'll make you agree that we unfortunately have to live with some compromises, if we want to save our civilization from deadly, relentless and ruthless enemies that are following no rules of civilized society and ready to exploit our democratic vulnerabilities. I think *keeping the purpose and consequences in mind* is a key to dealing with this dilemma. Paradox? No question! Some, I expect, will reject this point of view. That's okay—it's still a free Country. If you want to come to the roots of this sad paradox in better detail, we can do that a bit later."

"You, Deda, gave me a pretty good idea about where you are heading."

"Good! I hope, you aren't losing interest."

"Not at all."

"Well, I trust you didn't miss all these wonderful shades of color on the rim during the sunset. Now we have to get some sleep. Tomorrow I'll tell you a story of a Soviet 'saint'. I hope, this story will give you a vivid picture of the evil totalitarian environment created by Stalinism"

"Soviet saint? How can a determined atheistic society have a saint?"

"You'll see. Besides, communism is not as 'atheistic' ideology as you think."

7

Poster Saint

"In the U.S.S.R. social persuasion is a deliberately controlled force to secure individual conformity to the aim of the regime."

-John A. Armstrong.

"Everyone knew his name in Soviet Union, from the 5 years olds to senior citizens", I started when we took off south toward Sedona. "Hundreds and hundreds of pieces of art were created about this hero in different genres, from poems to operas. His portraits were seen in the picture galleries, on post cards, matchboxes and postage stamps. There were countless bronze statues of him in hundreds of cities around the country. The schools, libraries and ships carried his name. His posters were hanging in every class of the schools I attended. He looked slightly different every time, but who cared? The red tie of the Lenin's Pioneer was always there, aroun the neck of Pavlik

105

Morozov.

Even in 1982, during the 50th anniversary of Pavlik's death, the press called him a 'Martyr of Idea'. The place where he was murdered was enshrined. In atheistic Soviet press he was called a 'Saint'. No single child in the history of mankind was honored with such glory.

The official version of his heroism was that in the early1930s at the age of 13 he denounced his father to the Secret Police as 'an enemy of the Soviet State'. His father was arrested, tortured and sent to GULAG. According to propaganda, during that time, Pavlik helped to build communism in the Soviet Union. 'Enemies of the people, murdered him for that, and Soviet people declared him their hero, studied his biography in order to be like Pavlik Morozov."

"I can guess nobody has seen Pavlik's father alive."

"That's a correct guess. After the fall of communism in Russia numerous researchers studied the biography of Pavlik Morozov. Literally every one of the available sources gave different accounts about Pavlik's age, place of living, circumstances of his murder, even his appearance. No personal artifacts or photos of an actual living person, no documents about Pavlik Morozov have been found in the historical archives. The only source of information left for researchers was an account of neighbors and other 'perishable' witnesses, whose ages were often approaching a hundred."

"So, what was the real story?"

"The real story? Nobody cared about the real story, Myron. Adolf Hitler was very bold and honest in answering this kind of question: 'By means of shrewd lies, unremittingly repeated,' he said, 'it is possible to make people believe that heaven is hell – and hell (is) heaven. The greater the lie, the more readily it will be believed'."

"This bastard sure knew what he was talking about."

"Yes, he did and he practiced his philosophy to the fullest... Any way, there was a boy of 13 by name of Pavel Morozov, in the village Gerasimovka of Trans-Ural region of North-Western Siberia, who was murdered and then buried on September 7, 1932. His home was burned to the ground after the burial; his bones were exhumed years later under mysterious circumstances, put in the box, encapsulated in cement and reburied.

I have run my little research and translated to English a quite reliable, in my view, account of Russian investigative reporter Yuri Druzhnikov. I used the most interesting fragments and compiled the real Pavlik Morozov's story, the story of so called 'Communist Saint'. Here is how it unfolded:

Large print in local newspaper *Worker of Tavda* on

November 24, 1932 announced:

NOVEMBER 25, 1932, 6 PM, STALIN'S CLUB HALL, EXHIBITIONAL SESSION OF THE DISTRICT COURT, TRIAL OF MURDERERS OF PIONEER PAVLIK MOROSOV.

Tavda was a dirty and dilapidated tiny territorial center in the middle of the swampy North-West Siberian forest (Tayga), with a station crowded by railroad cars and platforms loaded with timber. A number of sparsely spread villages were situated around Tavda, with Gerasimovka among them, where the murder took place. Twelve hours West by train there was the city of Sverdlovsk, the regional center of Ural and a major transition point between European and Asian parts of Russia. The whole area around and to the East of Sverdlovsk was filled with hard labor camps and they were heavily guarded by the police and Special Forces of OGPU. This was the area of the first destination of millions of *kulaks* uprooted from their independent farms of Southern European Russia (Kuban') and Ukraine. The exiles were escorted by-foot; those strong enough not to perish on the way to Siberia would be placed in quickly built barracks or simply left to die while in the open forest waiting for shelter. The survivors worked to build a heavy industry based on rich mineral resources of Ural Mountains. They also cut trees in thick mosquito-infested Tayga. It was, Myron, the most brutal slave labor in the history of mankind, worse than what we saw in TV movies about Egypt, Rome, and Babylon. The weaklings would be shot—if they didn't die by themselves—and instantly replaced with new prisoners.

Originally, at the beginning of the century, the rugged peasants, running from the famine and war in Belarus, had settled in this area with some help from the Czarist government. They cleared the forest and set independent farms on the free land, raising cattle and harvesting potatoes and robust grains, barely surviving this harsh climate. In Stalin's time, the majority of them were labeled as *kulaks*. If they resisted forced collectivization, they were sent to the camps farther north to 'pioneer' tundra and mine rare minerals. Their farms and houses would be given to the 'lucky' and thoroughly subdued exiles from Kuban' and Ukraine, to help collectivization here after it failed there. This was a massive conveyor of displacement, intimidation, indoctrination, genocide and slave labor set by Stalin 'to fulfill the Five-Year Plan and build socialism in a single country'. Such is the background of this story."

"Dear God! Hard to imagine! I wish Hollywood would make some movies about that." Myron mused.

"Dreams, dreams! Hollywood's stories must have happy ending. Not in this case... Let's, though, come back to the events in Tavda. The clubhouse carrying Stalin's name, the large log building on the Stalin Street of Tavda, was freshly erected for the trial. The axes and hammers resonated in Tayga[1] day and night. Demonstrators with placards, including children of pre-school age were organized by the authorities and recorded for the press, demanding death to the "murderers". Dozens of speakers were set out for people unable to get inside the clubhouse. The wind-orchestra was lifting the spirit of the attendees and creating an almost eerie festival atmosphere. Vodka was sold without limitation. One of the attendees remembered: 'We were ordered early in the morning to be in Tavda for an urgent meeting. The police loaded the whole village population on ten open carts in 22 degree F below zero; and we found out only half way to Tavda what it was all about. When someone protested, they were offered two options: a meeting in Tavda with free buffet and vodka, or walking home and freezing to death".

The "mock" trial was to be held in the newly built Club while surrounded by troops of OGPU with rifles. Late in the afternoon, when the general meeting outside was over, the doors of the club were opened. Entrance was limited: each delegation was given a certain number of tickets. The

---

[1] Siberian forest, *Russ.*

clubroom for 600 accommodated twice as many and people were standing along the walls, sitting in the aisles and crowded in the back like herrings in a barrel. Tatyana Morozov, the mother of the two murdered boys—Pavlik and his younger brother Fedya—were sitting in the first row with her third son Aleksey on her lap.

The spectacle was so intense and impressive, that even half a century later the witnesses could remember every detail. The back wall of the stage was filled with red placards and in the middle of it hung a portrait of Pavlik Morozov, painted by the local amateur artist. To the left – placard: "WE DEMAND CONVICTION AND EXECUTION OF THE MURDERERS!" On the right – another slogan: "LET US BUILD THE AIRPLANE IN HONOR OF PAVLIK MOROZOV! GENEROUS CONTRIBUTIONS OF GRAIN IS ENCOURAGED!

The five accused were sitting at the center of the stage, guarded by the convoy. The defenders were Pavlik's relatives: Arseniy Kulukanov (the uncle, 70), Kseniya Morozov (grandmother, 80), Sergey Morozov (grangfather, 81) Danila Morozov (the cousin, 19), and Arseniy Morozov (the Pavlik's second uncle). The trial team of six,who had arrived from Sverdlovsk, were sitting on the stage behind a long table covered by red tablecloth with a morbid black fringe.

A later account of 'Worker of Tavda' made it abundantly obvious that this was not a trial in any traditional sense, but a spectacle with the assigned roles, interactions, buffet, and at the end a dramatic sentencing. With no material investigation, no presumption of innocence, no defending counsel, four out of five defendants were convicted of conspiracy and the murder of Pavlik and Fedya Morozovs. Propaganda put forth the motivation as a " *revenge for Pavlik's denunciation of his father, an enemy of the people in the people's victorious drive for communism'.* All four were taken out, lined up against the wall, and shot in front of the crowd."

"Quite like Nazi's trials and some modern executions in the Middle East?"

"That's right. The effect of this trial on the people's psyche was so dramatically corrupting and numbing that, when OGPU started later its massive campaign for collectivization and against the local 'kulaks' (independent farmers), sending them beyond the Arctic Circle or executing them on the spot, nobody raised any questions. Everyone was convinced that he was living among the enemy, and the Soviet government was here to help. You can guess, Myron, what was my and my classmates 'informed' opinion about Pavlik Morozov and his killers. Of course, he was my hero too."

"Quite a story! Who was his father? ...To be denounced by his own son! What had he done so bad?"

"Well, Gerasimovka was the most remote village in the Territory. It was so isolated by forest and swamps, making it inaccessible for most of the year, that during the Civil War the surrounding turmoil practically didn't touch the village. Even collectivization passed this place by, although authorities tried it and failed, meeting passive resistance. The authorities were annoyed, but almost gave up on that god-forsaken place. This village, Myron, knew no difference between Reds and Whites, supporters or opponent of Bolsheviks. The village never had any Lenin's Pioneer organization on its soil and had never seen the Red Tie associated with it."

"Really? How then could Pavlik be a 'Pioneer in the Gerasimovka Organization'?"

"He wasn't, Myron. The real story, as you will see, had nothing to do with the official government version. As we already learned, the more outrageous the lie, the more effective the propaganda and indoctrination."

"I believe this is what Hitler said in his manifesto *Mein Kampf*. So, who was he then?"

"Well, Pavlik was the first son of Trofim and Tatyana Morozovs. Trofim, a dedicated communist, was one of the very few Communists in the village, who fought on the side of Red Army against Kolchak. He was a war hero and chairman of the Village Soviet. The witnesses described him as tall, attractive, hard working and a fair-minded man. The family lived together in apparent harmony except for one 'little' fact: Pavlik Morozov didn't measure up in the least to his father's expectations. Villagers remembered him as a hooligan and school dropout; and our story would never have been born, if something unthinkable didn't happen to this family after years of harmony. One day Trofim gathered his things and left his family for another woman, 18-year old Ninka."

"Why the 'unthinkable', Deda?"

"Well, the husband could fool around, get dead drunk, beat his wife and kids, but leaving his family was 'crossing the line of the communistic behavior'… Any way, Tatyana couldn't get over her shame and was determined to get her husband back. Pavlik, who naturally hadn't been on good terms with his father, wasn't happy either. As an older son, he was now in charge of the cow and the horse they had in the household. Obviously, he liked neither to study at school nor to shovel manure.

So, the jealous wife, in an attempt to vent her rage didn't find anything better than threatening denunciation of her husband for, allegedly, selling forged documents to escapees. As a chairman, Trofim had access to such documents and, naturally, was vulnerable to blackmail. When the father refused to come back, Tatyana persuaded her son to contact OGPU. Soon after that, Trofim was arrested, beaten mercilessly, cried and begged for his son to take his words back. But the *meat-grinder* was already set in motion. The young strong man, a hero of the Civil War, was turned to a bloody skeleton after a few weeks of being beaten and was convicted to the GULAG. The forged documents, in the mean time, continued their way to the escapees after Trofims' arrest, basically proving him as guilty as any 'good Sibiriak' It was in the old Siberian tradition to help the escapees to get home; so a lot of people could be involved in this 'crime'. Stalin himself used forged documents when he escaped from Siberian exile in the Czarist time. Stalinism just once again demonstrated its ultimate hypocrisy.

One *almost funny* situation was common in the escapees' ordeal. Quite often the illiterate escapee would somehow obtain a blank pass document and try to find someone at the railroad station or some other public place to help him to fill it out. Of course, he would ask someone well dressed who looked intelligent. The rest would need no comment—all well-dressed people in the area were informants or even officers of the OGPU.

Ironically, according to Soviet law, the belongings of the

convicts and their families were subject to confiscation. So, Morozovs shot themselves in the foot on this account as well. They lost not only their man, who still somehow supported them, but all their possessions. Hated by their neighbors, they now faced a hard time of survival.

"Good school of wisdom for some, hah."

"Well, the Mother was richly rewarded later... But that's not an end to the story, Myron. Pavlik, in the mean time, found his new role of informer quite enticing. This was more to his nature. He started to spy on everyone he could and volunteered this information to the OGPU. People around were always talking about something *interesting*; so he would sneak behind fences and open windows.

Soon he was hired by the OGPU as a secret informer. At this point his neighbors had had enough. One day someone knifed him and his younger brother Fedya, when they went to the woods to gather wild cranberries."

"Horrible story!"

"Well, I wanted to give you a better flavor of this cancerous environment. I was born the year after Morozov's 'trial', when results of collectivization and forced expropriation had already killed millions. I grew up as a part of the system, marched in my innocent years like a marionette with a drum on my belly. This flavor sticks with me all these 30 years after leaving Russia.

Swimming in a sludge of blatant lies, brainwashing hypocrisy, and unthinkable brutality for a good half of my life, I've developed acute allergic reactions to the slightest smell of socialism, wherever I've encountered it; like a dog working on drugs and explosives."

"You mean you've met communists here in our country?"

"Thinking of some, Myron. They wouldn't admit it or wouldn't call it by its real name; but I can smell the scent even on the TV screen. For the less experienced ones like you, young man, here is some simple advice: beware of one who can't resist hugging and kissing a communist dictator, and one who is talking too much about his sacrifice for the oppressed and underprivileged. The excessive itch for wealth redistribution is also a good litmus test for the communist mentality."

"You are talking as if you don't want to share your fortune."

"Yeah, right! I don't remember in which pocket I've put it."

"I think you gave a pretty good idea about the origin and the nature of a totalitarian system. I have this funny taste in my mouth, Deda, as if I'd consumed a good bag of sour apples."

"They are sour indeed; but we are fairly close to Sedona, Myron, and I wouldn't mind catching my breath... Look at this canyon filled with pine trees. I miss them in my desert. The last time, when I was here in the late fall these trees below were covered with fresh white-blue snow. It was a fantastic panorama. Let's stop at this observation point, take a few pictures, have some lunch with the stuff we have in the cooler. I may need my hands off the wheel this time any way, just to help me in my argumentation. We are nearing a pretty controversial part of our conversation. It's isn't going to look pretty, Myron. The problem driving hell out of me is one that makes Western civilization extremely vulnerable for abuse by the ideologies following no rules of honest debate and conduct. I may get hot in my indignation. Please, keep chunk of ice ready, if I lose my composure. Before we come to that, however, I want to rid myself of one little handicap. Many call it: *Political Correctness*."

"I see… You are getting tough, Deda."

"You've heard nothing yet, young man; but again, please follow the logic."

8

Generation of liars

"Political correctness is a poison, a poison that has deviously infiltrated our society in some parts and been welcomed with open arms in others. It has taken the strongest and darkest feelings that we possess, and driven them deep into our soles. It has created a generation of liars."
-Glenn Beck. *The Real America*

"You called me 'tough'," I said, when we finished our lunch and came back to our topic. "It's easy to be tough when you are talking about villains of the past. Even Stalin can't reach you if you are too tough on him. Now we are entering the *real time territory* in our exchange of opinions.

As you know, the question of *how* to fight the totalitarian enemy with limited tools, available to democracy, is the most difficult one for conscientious people. It's a really thorny question. In fact, it is *the* question of the day. What is killing us is *a paranoid overuse of political correctness*, particularly, the asymmetrical approach from different parts of our society. This issue has been discussed by different authors from different aspects. Let me add one more.

Quite often, derogatory and racist remarks, addressed toward the silent majority, are ignored, but considered politically incorrect, when they come from the opposite direction. The fresh example is the racist anti-White outburst of Jeremiah Wright, the pastor of the TUCC mega church in Chicago. The silent majority sluggishly reacted to this asymmetry."

"Isn't political sensitivity to minorities the given.

"It is; but to my surprise, Myron, I've run into a funny paradox in my comparative study of two systems, Socialism vs. Capitalism. In the Soviet society *the service-provider (not consumer) is presumed to be always right*. With no competition and with chronic shortages of goods, salesmen and government officials didn't have to be politically correct and watch their language while addressing the person they served. So, among other things, I've got sick of all this insolence and said to myself: *I would rather live in a society, where the person*

120

serving me for my money has to be nice and politically correct, even if he personally doesn't give a hoot about me. If I don't like him, I go for service to somebody else. This was my reasoning; and what do you think, Myron? I bumped into a great idea of political correctness gone amuck right here, in America. *What happens, as someone said, is we start on this good path, with good intent, and we end up head first through the windshield. All that political correctness has done is shut us all up. It hasn't changed anybody's mind. Instead it's taken every opinion we have, it's taken every joke we have, and it's forced us to conceal them and hide them and bury them deeper...This is a dangerous place to dwell...Political correctness hasn't changed our hearts—it's just changed our faces."*

"Would you go back to Russia? They are different now."

"No, thanks... I don't know where Russia is going and when it is going to be there; but I'm sure I don't want to see the ugly face of a Russian past in the door frame of my American house.

If I can't call a corrupt leader of the Labor Union the crook and demagogue, can't call the racist leader of the NAACP the hate criminal, can't call a mosque in American Heartland the ideological center of Muslim extremism, even if it definitely is one, there is something very wrong going on in my beloved Country.

Our Constitution, Myron, has been our guarantee of *life, liberty and the pursuit of happiness* for about 230 years. It's strong, and nothing can easily negate it. But it has also commanded us to defend the Republic it represents; particularly, if its enemies don't follow the rules of a civilized society."

"Would you amend our constitution every time the conditions change?"

"Very carefully, and in a due process. It has been amended in accordance with historical realities many times. With all its amazing integrity it is much wiser than some think. It never hurts, however, to set some priorities in its application to someone who don't follow the law and the rules of civilized society. Have you ever dealt with a flood in your basement? What would you feel, standing up to your knees in the cold water, when in the middle of the chaos you hear your dearest one cry: 'Honey, the light bulb in the basement is so dusty; would you wipe it, please?' Well. Would you care, Myron, about the darn bulb, when you're wet, your butt is freezing, and your children's toys in the neighboring family room are in great danger?"

FDR made the painful decision to relocate a certain part of the population from Southern California, the hub of the navy operation against Japan, for the period of the war and settle them in internment camps in continental areas of the country; and a number of them indeed cooperated with the enemy. The Supreme Court upheld the constitutionality of this measure. So, when it came to the very preservation of society carrying our constitution, the Country had to choose between often difficult but sensible ways.

Conditions in hastily built barracks weren't exactly comfortable, but it was within international standards. In fact, the camp dwellers had often better food and services than the regular Americans around. The Japanese homeowners and farmers had an option to sell their property in California, or have someone tending it till they come back after the war. This action, although carefully crafted, has haunted us ever since. Many of the victims have been offered apologies and retributions, and our constitution survived this challenge."

"It just doesn't seem right, and I can't say I agree with what FDR did, even though I've always liked FDR."

"I haven't always; but in this case, I think, he acted in according to his Presidential job description—protect his Country first. After all, this is what our Constitution demands."

"How many people were interned?"

"About one hundred and ten thousand in the US and some in Canada…But now, Myron, please, compare this with the other side. Stalin 'interned' millions of independent farmers before WWII, sending them to death, because they interfered with the insane plans of forced collectivization. *Slave labor and extermination was the goal.* During the war he uprooted millions of people of different minority groups and sent them to Siberia and Middle Asia (with no preparation for settlement and no return after the war), when he suspected someone in their midst to be sympathetic with Nazis. He sent every Russian soldier, liberated from Nazi's concentration camps, to die in Siberia. Their only crime was that they were captured by the Nazis—Solzhenitsyn described it very vividly in his writings. The Nazis built their camps and crematoriums not for the temporary internment, as you can see. The Japanese army also committed massive genocide of the people in any area they captured. *Genocide and ethnic cleansing was the goal; and they followed no rules of the Geneva Convention.* Radical Muslims abduct, torture, and execute every one they can put their hands on - soldiers, policemen, civilians, businessmen, aid workers, missionaries, journalists, etc., and put their beheadings on public display."

"Do we honor the Geneva Convention? I don't mean to sound like Mother Teresa. Is there any way for us to show a good example and disregard what the villains are doing."

"Many thinkers, Myron, demand serious revisions of the Geneva Convention to meet current international situations. Today it serves only the villains. The major debate is about how to call the terrorists and other detainees - prisoners of war, gorillas, or common criminals; and we bend over backwards to provide dignified conditions for them. I'm not qualified for the judicial evaluation of any particular action, but you don't have to be a lawyer to see who is a perpetrator and who is in the defense. That's the whole difference."

"Two wrongs don't make a right, Deda!"

"To be one hundred percent correct in this asymmetrical fight, is to be one hundred percent stupid or dead, whichever option you like better. Besides, do you realize how much stench the proponents of pure stupidity or suicide would generate, if some of the successfully aborted terrorist acts had materialized?"

"Hard choice to make! ...Do you think we will ever come to drastic measures regarding the American Muslim community?"

"That would be a disaster, and I pray it will never happen; but I suspect, the radical, or at least unfriendly sentiments in the American Muslim community are still disturbing. There must be some solution short of drastic measures. It must be. But first, the American Islamic Community must show what side they are on. I'm afraid there is no way around that.

Denmark's recent story proves how disastrous it can be for the Country, when it puts political correctness first. Not long ago Denmark was proud of being probably the most liberal welfare state in the world. The immigration laws allowed the new Country residents and even illegal aliens to receive generous government assistance and citizenship almost immediately upon arrival. The strong aroma of cinnamon pastry attracted massive influxes of Muslim immigrants. They refused to culturally assimilate or speak the language of the Country giving them a shelter, and respect its laws, replacing it with Shariah in their isolated communities. It took less than a decade for them to decide that Danes should give up their rights to ridicule their beloved prophet or anybody else, if he is not to their taste. When Danes rejected the blackmail, the Muslim mobs showed who was the boss. To the Danes credit, the natives found enough brain cells to elect a conservative government, which immediately reversed this madness. By the new rules, each new immigrant had to show and practice an obligation to respect the Country's laws, language, customs, and make an honest living, before he was eligible for citizenship and all its perks. Good lesson for Denmark's neighbors that are often lacking those precious brain cells.

Australians found no problem in dealing with the bully's attitude of their Muslim communities. They have put their survival as a Nation *first,* and politely but firmly told anyone who doesn't like their Country's laws and culture to go somewhere else. I really don't know why we call the Aussies the 'Down-Under'—they are on so much higher ground than we are now. I hate to be melodramatic, but how useful would our beloved constitution be *if there wasn't anything or anybody left to follow."*

"I wouldn't like to be in position to make this kind of decision."

"I know, Myron; you wouldn't kill a fly. Tell me honestly, would you now, in light of the recent terror in England, where medical doctors were involved, be comfortable to seek the help of a medical specialist with a Muslim name, knowing that a number of them, although pledged *to heal but not to kill,* are actually your sworn enemies abusing their oath. Our softhearted 'defenders of freedom' are very outspoken and self-righteous, but when they were asked to tell frankly what would they do, if their own children fell victims of this asymmetry. 'Oh, this is different', or 'that's an unfair question', they would mumble."

"That's being kind of radical, isn't it, Deda!"

"Do you think it's too radical to defend yourself or your

friends and families? I wouldn't dance on the street, like many in Gaza, when innocent civilians in Israelis towns were shelled. No, I wouldn't wave my flag and drag mutilated bodies of the enemy fighters behind the trucks; and would never torture my enemies just in order for them to admit something they've never done, to denounce somebody they've never known.

The Prime Minister of Israel, Yehud Omert, expressed the difference between these two worlds pretty well in his address, right after the war with Hezbollah:

> *We do not dance on the roofs at the sight of the bodies of our enemy's children - we express genuine sorrow and regret. That is the monstrous behavior of our enemies."*

"So, what you think we have to do?'

"Well; some very prominent thinkers, for a starter, have spoken out about the need of profound adjustments to the Geneva Convention. Newt Gingrich, the guy having no conflict with common sense, said in his New Hampshire speech on the danger of this asymmetrical warfare against us:

> *What is truly frightening about the British experience is they are arresting British citizens, born in Britain, speaking English, who went to British schools, live in British housing, and have*

good jobs.

Newt Gingrich is talking here about the pure stupidity of fighting a war in "white gloves" against an enemy following no rules, gloves off. Listen to his suggestions that I completely subscribe to:

This is a serious problem that will lead to a serious debate about the First Amendment, but I think that the national security threat of losing an American city to a nuclear weapon, or losing several million Americans to a biological attack is so real that we need to proactively, now, develop the appropriate rules of engagement."

He goes even farther, with something I particularly liked and never thought about, something that doesn't require further fiddling with the American constitution, and something I consider a bold test of the world's determination to survive or go under:

I further think that we should propose a Geneva convention for fighting terrorism, which makes very clear that those who would fight outside the rules of law, those who would use weapons of mass destruction, and those who would target civilians are in fact subject to a totally different set of rules that allow us to protect civilization by defeating barbarism before it gains so much strength that it is truly horrendous. This is a sober topic, but I think it is a topic we need a national dialogue about, and we need to get ahead of the curve rather than wait until we literally lose a city.

What do you think, Myron? If the suicide murderer had his finger on the nuke, would he hesitate to trigger it? I would vote for a President with Newt Gingrich's credentials and determination. He demonstrated enough boldness and vision as a speaker, as a historian, as a thinker, when he with his *Contract* stopped the spread of socialism, imposed by the liberal Congress."

"I'll tell you something else, young man," I went on after a moment of hesitation. "If we actually lost a big city to a WMD smuggled through our porous borders, Capital Hill would tilt over with the body weight of the knee-jerk politicians, running for a solution; and then, for a moment, nobody would give a thought about the Geneva Convention. So why don't we get tough right now, before bad things happen? Let me be politically incorrect to its very end. I happen to think that we have squandered a perfect opportunity in the aftermath of 9/11. It should have been clear to our leaders that Americans tend to lose their tolerance for a war lasting more than a week and for heavy casualties, even when it comes to defending our way of life. So wouldn't it be smart to employ a much more decisive strategy, using every means we have, and finish with our sworn enemies before the liberal camps wake up in their tents."

"This, I'm afraid, would just open up a whole new can of worms."

"It would not. The idea that we have to wait for 'absolute proof" of the terrorist's finger sitting on a nuclear button is not just silly, it's flat out stupid. Knowing that this maniac wouldn't have hesitated a minute, wouldn't you rather have destroyed the Iranian nuclear facilities using some *fancy* weaponry, if regular means are not powerful enough? Exactly the same was definitely due for Bin Laden and his bunch of thugs in their Tora Bora foxhole. If what they used against New York on 9/11 is not a weapon of mass distraction, I don't know what it is. Am I too politically incorrect?"

"And let Genie out?"

"The Genie is already out--the modern terrorists don't need any justification for their heinous acts. President Truman took this step to avoid invasion of the Japanese mainland, which expected to be another Normandy slaughter, perhaps much bloodier... In the mean time, shouldn't we at least pay more attention at the airports to a person with an Arabic name and profile, than to a senior citizen with Italian or British ones, just like Israelis do?

Just recently I was ordered to take off my shoes two times—once at the check point and a second time at the gate. Do I look like a terrorist in my seventies? By the way, while we taking our shoes, watches, and belts off, terrorists are thinking about something else."

"This was the most politically incorrect speech I've ever heard from you, Deda."

"Good! You're not the only one who is gaining some clarity during the course of our journey. Me too."

"But I'm not sure about your quite radical ideas. You're asking for an international uproar."

"We are getting a bunch of crap from the UN no matter what we do."

"Your philosophy seems to me pretty frightening. There must be a less destructive way to defend our freedoms."

"Your suggestion?"

"I'm not sure."

"Welcome to the Liberal Club!"

"Tell me, Deda, how have we come to such a point, when we choose between political correctness and the survival of our Country?"

"Well, the Constitution of our melting pot was designed, among other good things, to protect the civil rights of every little chunk in this pot. Unfortunately, the honeymoon of the graceful majority with grateful minorities suffered quite a few interruptions along the way. Some ethnic, racial and political minority groups were radicalized in their demands for special rules and privileges and pushed the silent majority to accept the double standards of political correctness, which meant: what is okay for the 'powerless' minority to do, is a political taboo for the 'omnipotent' majority. The constitutional Bill of Rights was put on it head. Some radical groups have found it appropriate and convenient to slide very close to the edge of something that looks and feels like treason against the Republic, that protects them by its very laws. And they're getting away with it."

"That was a harsh statement for a former refugee and the member of a minority group."

"At least nobody can accuse me of hypocrisy."

"Touché! Have we covered today's agenda, dear Professor?"

"I bet you don't have anyone talking in such terms at your university."

"Probably not. What are we going to discuss tomorrow?"

"Tomorrow, on our way to my house, armed with some wonderful tools of open discussion, we'll begin our crusade against intolerance, zealotry, hypocrisy, and other bad things prevailing in some corners of our world of conscience today. I'm afraid, some historical materials I will present you won't like or even believe. Please try to be patient; I will be more than happy to go with you, Young Man, through some common points of confusion; in every detail I can master."

"All these things together?"

"No, but sometimes they go together.

For the beginning I want us to talk about the quasi-religious cult of communism and of radical liberalism. I'd like to join the ongoing debate on this subject from the perspective of my experience in Russia. There is a lot of confusion on this front, and they are, I'm afraid, severely obscuring our vision."

"Aren't you afraid to touch such a sensitive area like religion?"

"I am."

9

Ideology of Evil

God must be out of Russia in five years.

- Joseph Stalin.

Country without God is a terrible place.

-Margaret Werner: *Dancing under the Red Stars*

"Margaret Werner, remarkable women and the only American who survived Stalin's GULAG, was brought to the Soviet Union as a child by her parents, the American communists, who came to help Russia in building auto industry." I began next morning. "I remember the first and only one decent car, M-1, in Russia during the WWII, which strikingly resembled the one of the Ford's models.

Margaret's father was a believer in the *perfect social system*. During the hard time of depression in America, the unemployment-free Soviet Union looked like paradise. They didn't know that socialism can do everything but make people work both freely and productively. As a supervisor at the car factory in a city of Gorki he soon became disappointed with oppressive bureaucratic environment and humbly offered his help to fix some obvious problems. What a fool! For all his dedication and hard work he was thrown in KGB prison, tortured, sent to Siberia, and has never been heard from again. His wife and daughter were desperate to learn the fate of their beloved one. Only much later they found out that he died as a *Proud Communist.*

Margaret inherited an honest spirit of her father. At school, as a teen, she maintained her spirit. She didn't rebel; she just stood out like a soar thumb in a thoroughly brainwashed class and asked questions. Asking an honest question was a great sin in Stalinist Russia, only second to treason. It didn't take long for the authorities to decide that the best place for her would be much closer to her father. Due to her strong beliefs, character, and unbendable spirit she survived GULAG, was released after Stalin's demise, and after a long fight was allowed to come back to America. In her book, *Dancing under the Red Stars,* she shows how terrible a Country without God can be, and how much strength the believer can derive from his faith."

"Didn't Stalinism create its own sort of religion?" Myron interjected.

"Yes, it did. Stalin threw away the God of spirit and goodness, and created new polytheistic religious cult of personality with communism as a paradise and final destination."

"I see. Would you elaborate? I know that cults can worship everything from Christ to a devil."

"I would be glad to talk about that in a greater detail; but please keep in mind that it's a personal point of view of a man who lived and was thoroughly worked on in the environment of hostile to traditional religious beliefs. Bear with me—it's going to be one of those general deviations in our conversation... Let's have something to eat, take a deep breath and then continue along those lines."

*****

"I'll come back to communist ideology. Like many others I am convinced, Myron, that communism as *a nonreligious philosophy* is one of many myths of totalitarian world. Just like any religion, as I mentioned before, it has its gods, saints, heretics, devils, symbols and ceremonials," I went on. "The communist 'god' occupied the Lenin's Mausoleum for about seventy years. The heretic in the communist propaganda is someone who is against the dogma; and the *devil* of course is an ugly Yankee with a dollar sign on his thick belly."

"So, where is Pavlik Morozov in this classification?"

"The saint, of course, the martyr of idea. My story about Pavlik Morozov, Myron, served as a concrete example of how evil *the totalitarian system is, when wrapped into a pseudo-religious symbolism*, and how totally it can corrupt the human mind. I think we have to be able to recognize totalitarianism in order to fight it in any shape or form anywhere it takes roots. The line between moderate and extreme movement, between religion of mercy and the cult of evil can be very confusing. This is the place where the devil is hiding behind the saint, so to speak."

"Are you trying to compare different forms of religion systems, Deda?"

"Not exactly; I'm not a theologian. I just want to concentrate on similarities of the totalitarian political systems, which are using religious symbols as a shield or an instrument of indoctrination and domination over the masses. I think it's very important to be as clear as possible in this area before we go on."

"Wait a minute, Deda! Communism rejects deity and

considers its philosophy totally atheistic. Are you implying that communist ideology, wherever it takes root, is some kind of religion? "

"The radical doctrines, Myron, can be extremely opposite and parallel at the same time, using the same symbolism; but as you will see they end up meeting each other in *the same space called the totalitarian system of government.* They are cults and have nothing to do with conventional religion, which is mostly an innocent spiritual movement that we are accustomed to separate from the state and politics."

"Stop right here, Deda. How about king Henry VIII, the Supreme Head of the Church of England? How about Russian Orthodox Christianity, the royal instrument of oppression? How about the Catholic Church in the time of Inquisition? Was it a religion of spirituality, love and tolerance?"

"Very good point, Myron! I guess, for these specific periods of time I would be profane enough to qualify these religious institutions as totalitarian cults. I think any positive movement, religious or not, can slip for a moment or more out of its nature and basic teaching. In the Medieval time of epidemics and turmoil, the overwhelmed leadership of the church didn't find a better way than to support the totalitarian rulers or become totalitarian themselves. Big mistake! Many Popes apologized for this dark period. In a different way, the Catholic Church just recently transgressed again in the cover-up of pedophilia; and it's paying dearly for this evil manifestation of the 'human nature'. For centuries it will remember that lesson."

"Apology doesn't make it okay, does it, Deda."

" Haven't you, the nice and decent guy, ever screwed up in your life? If not, you're lucky. I don't think the church transgressions were encouraged by the Bible, just as I never taught you anything wrong."

"No, you haven't; but I guess His Holiness wouldn't like your intellectual exercises, would he? Jewish people were terribly persecuted by the Catholic inquisition…Why are you so quick to forgive them and be so harsh on Islam, for example?"

"The difference is in teachings. As long as religion has the real incentives to *never repeat its mistakes,* I think it is entitled to some benefit of the doubt. The Islam, though, is following today a Mohammedan edition of Koran, which professses intolerance and even hatred."

"I know, Deda; although I think we are often too lenient to repeated transgressors in our midst."

"You are correct. Do you know, Myron, who is the most lenient to the modern human transgressions?"

"Who's that?"

"Progressive judges, for instance. They let serial rapists, pedophiles, and killers walk and commit their crimes again. The liberal state of Vermont is particularly notorious for that.

I told you earlier, Myron, how communism operates and indoctrinates. Since it's not following common sense and human aspirations, it's using deceit as a tool of indoctrination. *The totalitarian religious cult is in itself a government*, and it doesn't need any state borders."

"Really? Haven't Jews in Diaspora governed themselves by Torah and Talmud, Deda? What's wrong with that?"

"Excellent point again, young man! Jews in Diaspora did use Torah and Talmud as Books of law and custom. But they didn't have any state of their own. The Book was their state and an instrument of survival as a nation and a culture. This tool helped to keep Jewish culture intact for an unprecedented two thousand years, and at the same time follow the laws of their hosts. When the same powerful instrument, however, is used aggressively for indoctrination, isolation, and subversion by totalitarian groups, regimes, or states, it's a pseudo-religious cult of ideology or personality. In short the basic litmus test is simple: *If the ultimate goal of the religious movement, documented in its teachings, is to perpetuate love, civility, morality and tolerance—it's a conventional religion; if the purpose is the propagation of hatred, fear, intolerance and brutality—it's a totalitarian religious cult. In this sense, Communism and radical Islam are in the same category."*

"Haw so?"

"Well, you know that every communist text book is a source of hatred toward Western way of life. Hatred mixed with envy. The Mohammedan version of Koran states clearly that the unbelievers are by definition in permanent state of war with Islam unless they are subdued or converted.

Let me come back. I want to give you a few more illustrations of the nature of this pseudo-religious cult called Communism, which is nothing but evil ideology.

Moscow has been a communist Mecca, the place of pilgrimage, since times of the Communist International, the global Marxist's organ of subversion. The books of Lenin and Stalin were the must-read-and-recite for every Soviet citizen, just like a Mohammedan Koran for Muslims, with an apostasy often punishable as a criminal offence. As in some other religions, the life of 'pious' Soviet citizens has also been focused on a glittering paradise; but only this paradise has always had some never-shrinkable *Waiting Period,* the never ending Five-Year Plans; just like a glimmer of light at the end of the long tunnel. So the Soviet citizens always asked *to be patient*.

The way communist propaganda treated the other religious beliefs has been particularly striking. The Stalinist regime had run the wild propaganda against any traditional religion, calling them 'the Opium for the People'. Churches were converted into libraries, recreational and sport facilities. One of the oldest Russian Orthodox Churches, a magnificent *Temple of Christ the Savior*, looking right over the Kremlin wall into Stalin's office, was demolished—Stalin apparently got tired of seeing this symbol of his seminarian past looking into his window. Later, after Stalin's demise, a huge outdoor public pool was built on this land. The pool was open even at the sub-zero temperature in the winter, and thick clouds of steam, coming up on quiet days, was seen from afar, symbolizing a deep sorrow of the defaced Holy Ground.

Just like radical Islam, Communism strongly discouraged friendly association with the foreign 'unbelievers'. Only highly trusted elite could associate with the Westerners. An involvement of the ordinary Soviet citizens with personnel of foreign embassies, for example, was monitored and severely punished. In years of Stalin's purges, any contact with the outside world was equal to suicide.

My maternal grandfather, your great-great-grandfather,

Josef Kemler, had two brothers who immigrated to America to escape a genocide incited by the czarist government. Grandfather used to receive some letters from them. At some point a little parcel with penicillin, then unknown in Russia, saved the life of my favorite uncle Serafim—he is still alive and lives with his family in Israel. Grandfather never shared his brothers' addresses with anyone in the family for a fear of getting us into trouble."

"How did they let your grandfather communicate with outside world?"

"I guess he was too old to bother... When we immigrated to America in 1977, I tried to find my cousins, with no success. The final records showed that Kemlers arrived to New York City on a steamship in summer of 1904."

"We may have a big family here, Deda. Too bad—it'd be fun."

"Yes, it would. Maybe some of them live in your neighborhood in New York under different names, and we had no chance to meet them.

Just like in a totalitarian Islamic state, the Stalin's pseudo-religious cult of personality dominated the life of society. Stalin had created the most oppressive environment in the human history. Hiring and firing on the jobs, which would carry some responsibilities, required an official Party approval. The membership to the Communist Party in these cases was a must. Every factory and institution was nationalized. To get on the 'black list' meant big trouble. Considering that nobody could run his own business in a socialist state, just to make living, you can imagine the magnitude of it, when someone was fired from the state owned institution. We could run beautiful Moscow Subway the whole day long, back and forth for five cents. The housing rent from the government, the only option scarcely available during Stalin's reign, costed less than ten percent of the income. The government could well make it free—the government was the boss and could do whatever it wanted."

"Education and health care were free, weren't they, Deda?"

"How could it not to be? The Soviet citizens were allowed to make just barely enough money to subsist between pay-days. That was the whole point of an environment of total control, the best way to enslave."

"Why there is no revolt?"

"There are dissident movements; but they are crushed before we know it. Totalitarian cult, Myron, is amazingly efficient in its propaganda and tactics. The 'Lenin Pioneers' organization and a Muslim Madrassas are the most effective mechanisms of indoctrination. I obviously didn't have a chance to sit on the floor of Madrassa with the Koran on my lap, but I remember myself marching in the military formations as the Lenin's Pioneer with red tie around my neck and a drum hanging on my belly, shouting *Hail to Comrade Stalin!, Hail to Communism!,* just like the *Hitler-Youth* in the Nazi's time, or like the joyful schoolchildren in Saddam's Iraq. Our schedule, our curriculum, and our war games had very distinct orientations – the Party, the Motherland, and an absolute indisputable loyalty to the government and to our Messiah, Comrade Stalin. So, if the seven years old could religiously march with placards in Siberia, demanding *death to the murderers*, why the kid of the same age from Madrassa can't be ready for a bomb belt in the name of Allah, especially, if his family doesn't mind?

Dehumanization of the 'unbelievers' in communism was imbedded into a children's consciousness as soon as they could speak; and government really liked to start 'public' education from the crib. In this environment, killing and mutilation of a dog or a human 'enemy' were equally desensitized. The terror, domination and torture was the modus of operandi. Genocide in the name of communism was worth a reward. .

The *unbeliever* was not considered worthy of being truthful to or honoring an agreement. This moral stand was expressed explicitly in the Mohammedan Koran. Likewise, almost every communist leader and negotiator faithfully practiced the same morality in diplomatic affairs. So much for a *free education!"*

"How about free medical care? It's on a top of our government agenda today."

"Take, Myron, all the pitfalls of a Canadian healthcare system and multiply it accordingly, and you'll get Soviet medicine. Modern medical equipment and medications were not for the ordinary citizens. The Soviet society adapted two sets of rules of ethics: one for the ordinary people and another for the elite, the priests of the cult. Special clinics, resorts and shops for communist bosses in Russia, the luxurious palaces for Saddam and his family and supporters, the massive Kim Jong Il's collections of very expensive wines and liquors at the expense of a starving population--all these are just a few examples of the Mafia-like totalitarian environment. But the most important thing is: The free health care, housing, and education are the powerful instruments of indoctrination and enslavement. "

"You cannot paint all liberals in one color, even if some of them are obsessed with an idea of equal rights and services. Leon Trotsky, Deda, seemed to demonstrate a great deal of integrity, didn't he? He was in charge of the

147

armed forces, but decided not to risk thousands of lives in order to save his own, when Stalin deposed him."

"That's exactly the point, my dear. The idealistic radical liberalism of the early Leon Trotsky had naturally evolved into a totalitarian cult of Joseph Stalin, the Russian Zeus; and when Trotsky finished his job and became too dangerous he was trashed and thrown out in the cold. Resemblance with the other totalitarian cults is striking…I can talk about that all day long, my friend."

"I am still wondering, what is the point of this sociological exercise of yours, Deda."

"Patience, Myron! Let's have lunch at this cute roadside place and then continue our journey into the world of fools and evils. You would see what I was leading to.

*****

We were following one of the oldest Western roads, a picturesque Route 66, the subject of countless ballads and fascinating stories. We'll skip the Interstate 40, and the '66' would lead us almost to the threshold of my house. We were crossing Golden Valley, approaching one of the most picturesque parts of Route 66 in Arizona. The road to Oatman, the tiny historic gold-mining town, sitting on the opposite, Western, side of the mountain range, was winding through the Black Mountains, opening incredible panoramas with every turn. I was behind the wheel, so Myron could twist his neck around, taking hundreds of pictures with his camera. The sun in the late afternoon was in a perfect sharp angle position to outline amazing diversity of the landscape. In about 30 minutes we approached Oatman with hordes of wild burrows walking on the single street of the town and munching on carrots from the hands of spectators. We were 15 minutes from home, but I suggested stopping at a local point of interest, the tiny hotel, where according to the legend, famous Clark Gable and Carole Lombard spent a honeymoon night. A small room on the second floor, where Clark managed to squeeze his large frame, has since been sealed as a relic. But the real attraction of this hotel was the age old dining room, known for its wonderful buffalo burgers and the walls stapled with thousands of one-dollar bills— every visitor was encouraged to staple one or more, signed and preserved for generations of buffalo-eaters. We also watched the Wild West Show on the dusty street, where a few guys were having a shoot-out for a little pouch of gold on the ground, until there was just one gunman left; and of course, it was the righteous town sheriff.

We left Oatman late afternoon. After little ride through the Route 66 we turned right on the Boundary Cone Road. A panorama of the Colorado River Valley with a green heaven of golf courses and agricultural fields opened in front of our eyes. Sun was approaching the mountain range behind the river. It painted thin layer of clouds on the horizon in every shade of the color red. Ten minutes, and we pushed the clicker at the gate of our community.

"Here we are, Myron." I pointed to a neatly arranged square. "Do you see this sign? It's Sun Lagos. Let's go through the gate."

We followed the road driving along the three communal artificial lakes. My house was against the back fence on the very summit of the community.

"Your roof, Deda, has a very distinctive Gothic shape."

"I thought so, too."

"Where did you leave your four-legged friend?"

"Apry is at the kennel. I'll pick him up tomorrow, they are already closed tonight."

"Let's, Deda, climb onto your celebrated roof-deck."

"Let's do just that."

"...Never seen the sky so huge! It makes me dizzy." Myron cried, his arms stretched out and his face lifted to the shower of newborn stars."

"Do you see, isn't that what I told you all along? On the roof we are much closer to the stars."

10

Vipers in the House

As a nation of freemen, we must live through all time,

or die by suicide.

Abraham Lincoln

The early morning was fresh—the best time to enjoy summer outdoors in the area. The sun had just popped from behind the Boundary Cone, a stand alone tall mountain on the forefront of the Black Mountain range. We were sitting with our coffee on the roof deck, surrounded by the mountains. The workers below, on a wide stretch of the desert that begins about 50 yards away right behind the wash system, were already busy, moving their heavy equipment and building a brand new *Sun Lagos* golf course. One huge excavator was digging the

151

artificial pond near the future Green. The others were spreading the topsoil, spraying it with water. Landscaped in forms of terraces descending toward our Wash System, this part of the course promised to be wide open to my backyard, and at the same time separated by the Wash, making me safe from the stray golf balls.

"Isn't it nice to go away from the life full of confusion, bury your head in the sand, and relax?"

"It certainly is. Next time you come, Myron, all this area behind will be green and hilly with some ponds and patches of yellow sand. One would like to hide himself and forget the world around..."

"Yes, it looks like you've won the lottery. Don't let, however, those oleanders to grow too tall and obscure your view. Let's come back to our subject, however. I'm intrigued. You spent almost the entire trip talking about history and the Bolshevik revolution, you skillfully blended socialism with some kind of religious cults... and then you lost me. Don't get me wrong—it was very enlightening; but what is your point?"

"Well, as you know, religion, when twisted, can be a powerful instrument of oppression and indoctrination. You'll be surprised how vivid this point will look once the picture is complete. Give me a little more time and you'll know what I mean... You see, the radical Left in Russia at the beginning of the 20th Century had been an originator of Bolshevism, which ultimately ended up with the world menace called *totalitarianism*. The reason was simple: I'm not afraid to repeat it: *The fundamentally unsound political system can be sustained only by force and indoctrination. In this sense Chairman Lenin and his CEO Leon Trotsky had no choice, but surrender it to a brutal totalitarian rule or lose their cause to common sense; and the pseudo-religious cult is an indispensible element for the totalitarian system to stay alive.*

Now let's see where we are today. The Soviet Union is gone. The oppressed satellites and ethnic enclaves began to enjoy their independence and their ties with the outside world. I hope Russia won't come back to socialism—they may be now on their slow way up regarding the famous evolutionary Tyler curve of democracy. The West is the one that is facing defeat of its democracy. Can we fight? Do we have it in us, or we are losing?

The question we have to ask ourselves is: *Who are our real adversaries in our fight with neo-totalitarianism, how to stop this slide, and how to win the war we didn't start?* Let's concentrate on this problem now. We need to be clear about that or we're destined to fight windmills with the success of the famous Don Quixote of La Mancha."

"Agree! It' given."

"It doesn't seem to be so obvious to some, however. Let's first address the facts and concerns of numerous people far smarter than your Deda about the role of a contemporary radical Left in our current struggle. I suspect, you're not going to hear much of this in your university; so brace up for some shocks."

"Well, well! Fire up."

"I'll start with a well-documented role of the American liberal elite in our Cold War struggle with communism. Please feel free to jump in, when you find it too unbelievable. It's a very touchy part of our discussion; and I'm glad we're not behind the steering wheel."

"Sounds intriguing!"

"I don't have to go far to begin. Glenn Beck in his book, *The Real America,* outlined the problem American communists had during the Cold War, when the evil nature of the communist ideology became increasingly clear to everyone blessed with some common sense. Here is what he said:

> *Now, the communists faced a dilemma. Who could they count on?' They couldn't rely on the Western working class to rise because it became 'too greedy and selfish' along with their capitalistic employers. So, the left wing came to the rescue through 'immiseration'. When you hear the theory*

that 'because we had much, they had none, or that you and I and Ronald McDonald are somehow responsible for the horrific living conditions in Africa, this is immiseration. It is as though those in the Holy World (of the Western liberalism) believe that if American conservatives would just change their attitudes, the communist ideologues or Muslim extremists would vanish—as would hunger, poverty, and racism.

Do you think, Myron, North Korea and Cuba would open up all their political prisons, and Iran would happily abolish its plans to nuke Israel off the face of the earth, as a prelude to the global Muslimization, if we were nice enough?"

"What slices of the American society are you talking about?"

"The majority of the *immiserates* are crowded on the American Pacific and Northern Atlantic Coasts among intellectual, entertainment and mass media elite. All these openly socialistic groups are pretty uniform in their sentiments. They dominate some professional fields, and the non-conformists among them have to be outstanding in their talent and perseverance to survive in this environment. The Michael Moores and Sean Penns of this world are having a free reign to exercise *the First* and collect their awards.

Europeans are well aware of their social and economic predicaments; and when they are overdosed with socialism they all call conservatives back. The time for a sensible attitude in Europe, overwhelmed with illegal immigration, is rapidly running out."

"The radical left wing crowd in America is in a tiny minority. Can they be ignored; left alone to exercise their rights? Do you, Deda, consider them traitors?"

"Sure they could be ignored, but not when they hurt our soldiers on the front line, or spew blatant slender. I would be careful, though, in applying the term *traitor* easily to American citizens—it carries heavy weight. Leon Trotsky was an idealist and a brilliant egomaniac; so was Norman Mailer, the apostle of American liberalism, but I wouldn't call either of them 'traitors'. And do you know who the liberal most dedicated political foot soldiers are?"

"Who's that?"

"The guys having no idea where China is; the crowd of lumpen-proletarians who never held an elementary book of history in their hands; or simply a mob crowd, the engine of anarchy and a platform for political corruption. Take the most recent battle between liberal Labor Unions and freshly elected moderate government in Wisconsin. If not for the strength of our Republic, it would end up with a

Bolshevik type of revolution."

"It seems like you are determined to exercise your rights to be controversial, aren't you, Deda?"

"And politically incorrect when it comes to standing for our Republic of Law. If late leaders of the Soviet Union were asked how to defeat America, they would respond: 'We can not. They must defeat themselves'."

"I think, that's quite a stretch."

"Not at all! Abraham Lincoln outlined the concept of *the Enemy Within* in the time of Civil War quite similarly by saying:

> *All the armies of Europe, Asia and Africa combined, with all treasures of the earth in their military chest, with Bonaparte for a commander, could not by force take a drink from the Ohio, or make a track on the Blue Ridge, in the trial of a thousand years... If destruction (were) our lot, we must ourselves be its author and finisher.*

I would humbly bow to every single word of this statement of the great thinker and patriot. And they are very timely today, Myron."

"These are very strong accusations. You'd better elaborate if you go public?"

"Well, let's look at a few examples. Back in the mid 1960's, the Florida congressman Albert Herlong presented an official list of steps required to defeat capitalism, The list was originated in Russia by the Communist Party and KGB under the name: 'Goals of 1963'. This list contained 45 steps. I'll name only some of them, which have in a prevailing view been (or nearly been) accomplished with the help of the American Left Wing establishment and special-interest groups, before Ronald Reagan reversed this process. Here is what the KGB wanted the American Left to help them with:

1. US acceptance of co-existence as the only alternative to atomic war.

2. US willingness to capitulate rather than to engage in atomic war.

3. Develop an illusion that total disarmament by the US would be a demonstration of 'moral strength'.

4. Extension of long-term loans to Russia and Soviet Satellites.

5. Provide American aid to all nations regardless of Communist domination.

6. Recognition and an admission of Red China to the UN.

7. Set up East and West Germany as separate states in spite of existing agreements for the free elections under the UN supervision.

8. Allow all Soviet Satellites individual representation in the UN.

9. Get control of the schools. Use them as transmission belts for Socialism. Soften the school curriculum.

10. Use student riots to instigate public protests against programs and organizations which are under Communist attack.

11. Infiltrate the press. Get control of textbook review assignments, editorial writing, and policy-making positions.

12. Gain control of key positions in radio, TV and motion pictures.

13. Eliminate all laws governing obscenity by calling them 'censorship' and a 'violation of free speech and free press'.

14. Break down cultural standards of morality by promoting pornography and obscenity in books, magazines, motion pictures, radio and TV.

15. Infiltrate the churches and replace revealed religion with 'social' religion.

16. Discredit the Bible and emphasize the need for intellectual maturity, which does not need a 'religious crutch'.

17. Eliminate prayer or any phase of religious

159

expression in the schools on the grounds that it violates the principles of 'separation of church and state'.

18. Treat all behavioral problems as psychiatric disorders, which no one but psychiatrists can understand or treat.

19. Discredit the family as an institution. Encourage promiscuity and easy divorce.

20. Emphasize the need to raise children away from negative influence of parents.

21. Create the impression that violence and insurrection are legitimate aspects of the American tradition; that students and special interest groups should rise up and make a 'united front' to solve economic, political, and social problems."

"You made it all up, Deda. You have just compiled all of the 'concerns' we hear from the conservatives nearly every day on the radio and on some TV channels."

"Just to the contrary. We are talking about them, because they are already here; and I can extend my congratulations to our Secular Progressives. Twenty points out of a wild list of forty-five had been quite an accomplishment for the Soviet propaganda machine. The KGB, I am sure, was very pleased...I didn't make up a single word of this list; neither did congressman Herlong. If you looked around intelligently, you would find these characteristics in the everyday reality of our life, in the very fabric of our society."

"If they don't do any good to our society, why do you think Progressives cling to them?"

"I lived with this question in Russia, and I asked myself over and over again: 'Why is America buying this crap?' The communist propaganda in my time in Russia was diabolically focused on this agenda in its application to the 'American Imperialism' and gloated at the signs of weakness of democratic system. What a 'terrible pity' that this communist *Giant on the Clay Legs* had disintegrated before it oozed out and completed its entire ambitious agenda!"

"You are getting sarcastic, Deda. Enjoying yourself?"

"No, Myron, there is not much here to enjoy. The monster is gone, leaving behind some stinky KGB 'excrement'. The former communists are ruling now over the remains of this giant, and stretching their limbs again, but are having difficulties to reverse the history.

What's amazing to me, though, is that during my time in America, I've been sensing—on and off—a very familiar smell emanating from some corners of our society, same call for collectivization, expropriation, redistribution, and socialized healthcare, childcare, and education. Putin's

KGB buddies are an excellent source of advice in this area. They are aging but still in good shape and looking forward to a new generation of fools and liars."

"Hm...Why don't we distribute wealth more equitably; what's wrong with that? "

"Everything, Myron, just about everything."

"Well, start with healthcare."

"All right; this topic is perhaps the closest to the heart of many people. I believe I've already told you about how my uncle was saved by American penicillin, the common antibiotic not available in Russia, or available only for the elite. Here is another example. My 75 year old mother, your great grandmother, broke her hip trying to do what older people are not supposed to do—climbing the chair— and ended up in the hospital. She was left alone in the hospital room in pain for many hours. It took some bribe for the doctor and for the nurse to persuade them to pay some attention to my mother. There is no end to similar examples in the environment of a socialized healthcare system."

"Isn't it typical of just a totalitarian environment?"

"No, Myron. Canada and Great Britain are not totalitarian countries by any means; they just happened to have socialized medical care; and their citizens often have to wait for more than a year for some critical medical procedures. In many cases they travel to America and pay full price for the life saving procedure."

"Can't argue with facts; but how about child fostering and education? American single moms have to choose between staying home on welfare, or working and leaving their children on the street or behind locked doors. American education is in even a more pathetic situation. Lots of public high school graduates are actually illiterate."

"You are correct, Myron, about single mothers; but they should think about that before she become one— Capitalism is about responsibility; and besides, I know many who are deliberately planning for welfare. At least, the social structure shouldn't encourage single motherhood. Elmer, your step-uncle, had a girlfriend who happened to be single mom of a spoiled 7 year old girl. She was chronically unemployed. Elmer tried to convince her to find a job. He was ready to arrange his work hours, so they can take care of the child. He even found her a job at the WalMart store. She showed up to work for a few days and quit: 'Why should I break my back. Welfare gives me more money and benefits'.

Education, however, is a very interesting case. The current chaos in American education, lack of discipline and responsibility is, in my opinion, a result of liberal policies of permissiveness professed by Dr. Spock. The social science doesn't follow mathematical formulas, and it takes often more than single life of its originator to prove it right or otherwise. And I'm not sure who Dr. Spock was first, the scientist or spokesman of radical liberalism.

The educational system in totalitarian countries is far from liberal. An education there is a critical part of propaganda and indoctrination. The totalitarian government readily takes a child basically from the crib and minimizes a parent's involvement in raising them. Child goes through a selection of the fittest for the ruling government elite and critical industries. The rest of the children are potentially a state owned 'workforce'. Discipline and political conformity are the major emphasis in this system. Students, during my time in school, didn't argue with a teacher and had to hold their trips to the restroom until break time. As a positive side effect of this system, the totalitarian school produced a better educated graduate, even those not selected for the elite programs. There was no illiterate high school graduate in my time in Russia. A lot of Russian immigrants of my generation are doing quite well in America, even without initial English and social skills."

"Better than American Ivy League graduates?"

"Some are, some are not; but in an average the totalitarian school produces much more comprehensively educated graduates. Don't get me wrong. I'm not advocating a socialized or brutalized education. Discipline and responsibility, however, is the key in any education."

"So, government involvement sometimes produces positive results, doesn't it?"

"You are a smart butt. Of course, the totalitarian system has strong survival instincts. It replaces incentive with a fear of reprisals, productivity with an effort to concentrate endemically very limited resources at the key points, abandoning the rest."

"Do you really think, Deda, that America can fall into Communistic crap? Do you think Americans will buy into it so easily?"

"Not intentionally; but due to a serious lack of education in history. I had even run my own little random survey in the course of my first book promotion. I asked my potential readers a simple question: 'do you know who Stalin was?' Almost a half didn't know anything about the monster who killed 50 million of his own people and terrorized the world for decades."

"Wow!"

"That's right; and results of this ignorance can be devastating, considering that the forces promoting Socialism are always around, like a viper ready to uncoil and strike."

"You make it sound like a conspiracy in treason."

"Well, as I said before, I would be careful to throw around words like that; but let's see how, according to some pretty serious accounts, the radical Left of the mid 20th century exercised an aggressive push of communism, and how determined are Secular Progressives now in their fiddling with an idea of Neo-Totalitarianism.

Ann Coulter in her explosive book *Treason* —she really did use this term—compiled in a heavily documented fashion an astonishing indictment of American communists and radical liberal elite in their pro-Stalinist role during the period around WWII; and she was following an evolution of their role up to the present time. I find this stuff both very convincing and hard to contemplate—so unbelievable it is."

"Are you talking about the McCarthy probe? McCarthyism was the darkest period of American history."

"Yes, Myron, it certainly was, but not in the sense we were led to believe. Surprise? Let's go briefly through Coulter's findings and arguments. I admit, I would never dare get so bold."

"Are you trying to say that senator Joe McCarthy was right in his Witch Hunt?"

"I am not saying anything, and I wouldn't necessarily subscribe to every word she said in public; but nobody pulls her to court, so she must be right somewhere. Let me just recline in my Lazy Boy, relax, and turn you against Ann Coulter as *her* devil's advocate for a change. Try your wits—she's sharp like a razor and has earned a lot of enemies in the radical Left circles. It wouldn't be to her safety to make it up; so she has to back up every statement. I want to see how you're going to score against her."

"Go right ahead!"

"Okay, buckle up. Here is her book. I will quote some fragments of it, and we'll see what you think:

In June 2002, an American-born Muslim named Abdulla Al-Mujahir was arrested on charges of trying to build a dirty bomb. Most Americans were worried about terrorist's taking Lower Manhattan out. But New York Times was worrying about an outbreak of the 'New McCarthyism'. The days after 9/11, when the Ground Zero was still smoldering, Professor Eric Foner of Columbia University made a statement: 'I'm not sure which is more frightening - the horror that engulfed New York City or the apocalyptic rhetoric emanating from the White House'.

Isn't that an unbelievable statement? I honestly have no idea what was on the radical liberal minds in the middle of the last century, when they lined up with communists in a formation of the largest and deepest espionage ring in our country ever. I'll give you a little summary of the well documented events according to Ann Coulter's account; and you can sleep on them."

"The espionage ring? You are kidding me, Deda"

"I know. You may find this stuff too heavy and hard to believe; but I'm afraid you have no choice but to suffer a bit of a shock. It's a key element of our arguments for peace and preservation of our Republic. The legacy of Trotsky's Permanent Revolution is very much alive... Let's come back to Ann Coulter: In 1938, in the middle Stalin's purges, the notorious American communist Whittaker Chambers broke with communist party. With great distress 'Chambers came to the realization that all his life he had been working on the side of evil—the terror, torture, fascism, and death'. It was a time when scores of American communists, trapped in Russia while running in droves to help Stalin in fulfilling his Five Year Plans, got their taste of totalitarianism. I told you about the fate of Margaret Werner's family. Brought to Russia as a teenager by her father, she was one of many innocent victims of the American radical Left's fascination with Stalinism.

For Chambers this move was equal to suicide—communists just like Islamic Jihad or any other Mafia for that matter never tolerated apostasy. The moment he learned about the Stalin-Hitler Pact and the Nazi's march into Poland, he got an audience with Adolf Berle, the FDR's assistant secretary of state, and spent hours in 'detailing the Communist espionage network he had been a part of. Among more than two dozens Soviet spies working for the Roosevelt administration was Alger Hiss, a top State Department official, and his brother Donald Hiss'. When Berle brought this information to President Roosevelt, he was laughed off and dismissed as a fool and liar. Despite that information, when the time came in Yalta to divide the world between superpowers after the WWII victory, guess who was the Presidents major adviser."

"Who?"

"Alger Hiss... Moreover, Dean Acheson, then the undersecretary of the Treasury, also dismissed Chamber's confession, and 'when he was appointed as assistant secretary of state, he momentarily requested Donald Hiss as his assistant'.

In 1948 the newly formed *House Un-American Activity Committee* (HAAC) decided to ask Hiss some questions. Chambers testified against Hiss; but in spite of inconsistent testimony Hiss walked. New York Times qualified Hiss' performance as a 'smashing success'. Chambers, however, was the one who got into deep trouble, being accused of slander. Only Nixon believed Chambers' testimony and tried to save him… 'Almost fifty years later, upon disintegration of the Soviet Union, the release of decrypted Soviet cables proved indisputably that Hiss was a Soviet spy.' The New York Times was very surprised, *even shocked.*"

"I'm still confused, Deda. Is Ann Coulter actually accusing all American Left of treason?"

"Not any Left, Myron, but the Radical one; and they haven't change their ways. Besides, confusion is a first step to enlightenment. You can only guess, Myron, how much damage to Eastern Europe, Asia, the American foreign policy and its position in the world these guys brought in a course of years of espionage. You can see what kind of advice the ailing President had been provided at the Yalta Conference, if he had no idea who his advisers were. No wonder that his *good old friend Uncle Joe* got out of this conference smiling and gently caressing his bushy mustache. Hundreds of thousands of American soldiers, who gave their lives to defend our country and Europe, were betrayed, and as a result, millions of new subjects in Eastern Europe were handed to Stalin on a golden plate for 45 years of slavery. 'I like old Joe (he meant Stalin, not McCarthy), Joe is a decent fellow', was President Truman's sentiment. What do you think, Myron? Shocking?"

"Hard to believe! ...You still didn't enlighten me about McCarthy's role, Deda.."

"Well; much later, when the espionage activity was so obvious, that it inflamed public uproar, Joe McCarthy started his methodical investigation of, as he said, 'a conspiracy on a scale so immense as to dwarf any previous such venture in the history of man'.

'Many accounts show that Joe McCarthy was as much a darling to the general public, as he was a villain to the radical Left,' Ann Coulter wrote... So, what would you, Myron, do, if you faced such an overwhelming set of facts, like McCarthy did? Would you ignore it, or rather risk to being vilified when you acted upon it?"

"Joe McCarthy as a 'Good Guy'? I have to really struggle with these words coming together. This is not a prevailing sentiment in New York intellectual circles."

"That's because the New York Times fed the information. I think this was a living example of the utter pervasiveness of indoctrination prevailing at this time. Just imagine for the sake of argument, Myron, that today's Federal Bank, the offices of the Secretary of State, Secretary of Treasury, and the office of the President himself are infiltrated by spies up to the level of the second in charge. I think you would agree that Joe McCarthy's bold probe was pretty much overdue."

*****

"Do you really believe in this heavy stuff, Deda." Myron asked me after a few minutes of silence.

"Wouldn't you? Naturally, I didn't have any access to the sensitive or even any public information while living in Russia. Now I've seen it on both sides like on a wide screen; and how many of us are still alive to express what we feel? ... Any way; let me go very briefly through the evolution of the Secular Progressive movement after a tumultuous WWII.

After the Hiss debacle, the execution of Julius and Ethel Rosenberg, and McCarthy's probe, causing some disorientation in the liberal movement, the American radical Left had received their above-mentioned 45-point KGB list to act upon. They failed to respond to the Korean War--American victory in Korea was too impressive in establishing a solid fore post of democracy on the Korean Peninsula. Then Vietnam came. 'In spite of 80 percent of the American public support of this war,' Coulter wrote, 'the crowd of youthful onanists, smoking pot in their Berkeley dorm rooms', prevailed in bringing the war on the brink of disaster; and the inept handling of it by

Lyndon Johnson made his defeat in the re-election inevitable.' So was the American defeat in the war.

President Nixon tried to end the war honorably, but blundered in his second term campaign. Using hysteria over Watergate as a cover, congressional Democrats openly turned their backs on the South Vietnamese, leading to a total communist conquest of Indochina'—and you know, Myron, how many millions of innocent people were massacred in the aftermath.

Would you like to get an idea about the overall price that humanity paid for our complacency about global totalitarianism? Remember that along with communist terror of the first half of the last century, every death, which occurred during World War II, was the responsibility, ultimately, of the totalitarian Fascists of Germany, Italy, and Imperial Japan. Any quibbling about Dresden or Nagasaki is pointless: they would not have suffered a single war-related death had the Fascists been silenced by their own people. Here is a rough compilation of the totalitarian toll:

Deaths during Lenin era of Russian Communism
(including Russian Civil War): 9,000,000 (est.)
Deaths due to European Fascism: 42,000,000 (est.)
Deaths to Asian Fascism: 15,500,000 (est.)
Deaths due to Stalinist Regime in Russia (including

Ukrainian Genocide): 20,000,000 to 50,000,000 (est.)

Deaths during Chinese Civil War: 2,500,000 (est.)

Deaths during Communist China (Mao's Regime 1949-1975): 40,000,000 (est.)

Deaths during China's Nationalist Era (1928-37): 3,100,000 (est.)

Deaths during Korean War: 2,800,000 (est.)

Deaths during North Korean Regime (1948 - present, not including Korean War): 1,633,000 (est.)

Deaths during Vietnam War (1960 - 1975): 3,500,000 (est.)

Deaths during Cambodia's Communist Khmer Rouge Regime(1975-1978): 1,650,000 (est.)...

The numbers are staggering, aren't they? Beyond human comprehension! Truly, I can't wrap my head around numbers this high. Yet, each of those gargantuan numbers represents human beings. Millions upon millions of humans, snuffed out, slaughtered, wiped off the face of the earth, for the sake of Communism, Fascism, or, of late, militant Islam. These were men, women, and children, old and young, gone forever because of power-hungry zealous fanatics, whose philosophies they don't even try to hide."

"These numbers can't be confirmed, Deda."

"So what! The numbers are mind-blowing, even if the accuracy of some can be disputed; but this is beyond the point; there should be no doubt in the evil nature of totalitarianism."

"This is hard to unimagine. I know now where your allergy to communism is coming from."

"Yes. As I said before, I'm like a dog working explosives. Anyway, things in America were going well according to the KGB agenda after defeat the Vietnam War; and as you can see, a lot of bad things can happen to a country, when it shows weakness and disarray. The bad guy is always there to take advantage of an opportunity... But here, Myron, came a new Oval Office occupant, the tall and handsome cowboy, an ordinary actor but brilliant politician, the man of faith, principles and a great sense of humor. He told the radical liberal crowd to screw themselves and knocked the Soviet monster off of its clay feet."

"It sounds like a fairy tale. You seemed to be enjoying the end of it."

"I wish it were the end of it. A peaceful majority has always been a silent one, and the radical minority quite often owns them.

You know, very few people in Germany were Nazis, but many enjoyed Nazi's slogans after years of disarray, and many more were too busy to care. Then, before Germans knew it, Nazis owned them, and they had lost control, and the end of the world had come.

Communist Russia comprised Russians who just wanted to live in peace, yet the Russian Communists were responsible for the murder of millions. The peaceful majority was irrelevant.

China's huge population was peaceful as well, but Chinese Communists managed to kill staggering tens of millions.

The average Japanese individual prior to WWII was not a warmongering sadist. Yet, Japan murdered and slaughtered its way across Southeast and mainland Asia in an orgy of killing that included the systematic murder of Chinese civilians; most killed by sword, shovel, and bayonet.

History lessons are often incredibly simple and blunt, yet for all our powers of reason we are missing again the most basic and uncomplicated point: Peace-loving Muslims have been made irrelevant by their silence. Peace-loving Muslims will become our enemy if they don't speak up, because they will awake one day and find that the fanatics own them, and the end of their world will have begun.

It's the fanatics who march. It's the fanatics who wage any one of 50 shooting wars worldwide. It's the fanatics who systematically slaughter Christian or tribal groups throughout Africa and are gradually taking over the entire continent in an Islamic wave. It is the fanatics who bomb, behead, murder, or honor kill. It's the fanatics who take over mosque after mosque, converting them into headquarters of terrorism, and it's the fanatics who zealously spread the stoning and hanging of rape victims and homosexuals. The hard quantifiable fact is that the complacent majorities of Muslims are cowed and extraneous.

Finally, at the risk of offending someone, I sincerely think that anyone who rejects this as just another political rant, or doubts the seriousness of this issue, is part of the problem."

"It's quite a manifesto, Deda. I feel you can talk about that forever. I don't mean to be complacent, but I'm hungry. Let's see what is there in your fridge."

11

Mysterious Evolution

"The knowledge of truth as such is wonderful, (but) here we face the limits of the purely rational conception of our existence."
- Albert Einstein. *Princeton Theological .Seminary, May 19, 1939*

.

"OK, let's assume you are right about the radical Left. I still have difficulties to fathom the forces, driving them in such treacherous waters." Myron went on after the break. "What is their philosophical basis? Their Ideology. Marxism? Leninism? It can't be; this philosophy has discredited itself forever. Is it a new phenomenon, or the old one under different name? What is the goal? Would you enlighten me?"

"Well, I can give it a try. Many books are written on this subject, and almost each of them seems to have a merit... You remember, Myron, our earlier conversation about total state control over its subjects as a major feature of socialism. The effective way to achieve that was creating the pseudo-religious cult of personality as a communist alternative to a Judeo-Christian Western tradition. Traditional Christianity with its anthropocentric views, its respect for human life, the ideas of Deity, afterlife, and an intelligent design has been an anathema to totalitarian ideology, preaching free manipulation of human genetics as common and the creating of a superior race by the forced selection of the fittest, while eliminating the physical and political misfits. Stalin and Hitler used concentration camps and mental institutions as common tools. Charles Darwin was one of the Major Prophets in both Communist and Nazi pseudo-religious cults. The Theory of Evolution was regarded in socialist Russia as a pinnacle of biology. Hitler cherished Darwin and used the *Theory of Evolution* in his book, the Nazi bible, *Mein Kampf,* to justify genocide and ghastly experiments on humans. So, Charles Darwin was ironically but not surprisingly an icon for both totalitarian systems."

"Do you think Darwin meant to have his theory used like that?"

"I don't know. Maybe not, but that's beyond the point. It's very convenient, it suits well into totalitarian ideology."

"Are you trying to equate our Secular Progressives with

179

Communists and Fascists just because they accepted the theory of Evolution?"

"Patience! You're smart enough. Try to figure it out. One can only hope that they just don't know what they, or at least the majority of them, are doing. Besides, I grew up as an Evolutionist in Russia. Considering any other point of view was taboo. Marxism rejected the philosophical idealism and metaphysics. The idea of *intelligent design* and superiority of a liberated mind over matter was ridiculed by communist propaganda, and often considered the sign of insanity, serious enough to grant you a bed with restraining straps in the madhouse. How do you think it was possible for me to contemplate any other alternatives, even as an abstract intellectual exercise, considering the years of brainwashing? Materialism and atheism were solidly in my blood.

The Western Progressives, presenting a human as just one little step from the ape, could justify behavior, emulating an ape's explicit sexual performance in front of amused spectators at the Zoo. Theory of Evolution is very convenient for the radical crowd having no idea what to do with decency and morality. Just recently, Myron, I saw some TV clips from one of San Francisco's parades showing in public literally what I'm talking about. High school teens are readily emulating this behavior in public places and on school buses."

"Are you rejecting an idea of evolution in general?"

"Not at all! The evidence of natural selection and gradual positive mutation within species in response to changing environment is there; but many serious scientists maintain that millions of multi-cellular animal species on their record appeared in the fossil database about 540 million years ago. All these structurally very different, and at the same time functionally very similar species appeared within a few million years around this era. On the background of 540 million years, this period of time can be considered within a margin of error in the fossil age measurements, and may very well be interpreted as an instant in time. Who put them on a map in virtual instant, many of them with all those sophisticated eyes and other organs, which are still impossible to match by any technology we have now? Who could create a single cell, the building block of life, with a capacity no supercomputer can compete with?

Trial and error random mutation? Are you kidding me? One of the most prominent spokesmen of Secular Progressives, Richard Dawkins, couldn't explain that. All he could do is to demand the hard prove of Intelligent Design. What if we live in different dimension and don't have an access to Him and His ways while we are alive?"

"What is the point?"

"The point is that this revolutionary development in life on the earth is really devastating news for the Secular Progressives trying to prove that secular truth is the only truth. But we know how the Bolsheviks created 'scientific' facts in the political arena. If Lenin said so, it was an indisputable fact. If you disagreed, it was too bad…for you! This is exactly how Darwin's followers were conducting this debate. I happened to be a scientist, Myron, and my question is simple and straight forward: Show me the undeniable fact of a gradual mutation of amoeba or even a monkey into a human, here on earth, not in Heaven, not in some different dimension, and I will think about it; but until then I am open to different alternatives. My toy poodle Apry told me: 'I'm not so stupid to become a human—you never know what you're gonna' get. I'm quite happy in my beautiful apricot skin, Master'."

"Is that what he said?"

"Just about… By the way, Myron, to the great Darwin's credit, he came out with a real scientific standard for the test of his theory: *'If it could be demonstrated that any complex organ existed which could not possibly have been formed by numerous, successive, slight modifications, my theory would absolutely break down.'*

Thank you, Dr. Darwin, you're an honest man! I know it's not fun when your theory breaks down, especially if it proves to be wrong on the millions of samples. Radicals have taken you out of context. They're just using you. There is in my view absolutely no possibility for the unimaginably complex system like living cell to evolve by trial-and-error mutation even in billions of years. Never mind an organ like eye or brain, in a virtual instance.

Not to the Darwin's followers, though! They very conveniently ignored his profound and honest statement. Ironically, the great advancements of science after his death provided plenty of evidence of the earth 'instantaneous population' by the animals, and have left his users with two choices: suggest a ridiculous idea of implanting the millions of different species 540 million years ago by the extra-terrestrials, or accept a possibility of *their absolute anathema - the Intelligent Design.* 'We cannot allow a divine foot in the door,' the Harvard population biologist Richard Levontin said with a great deal of anxiety. This was a very 'scientific' statement, in the best traditions of Stalinism.

In his book 'Life After Death', fascinating in its iron logic, Dinesh D'Souza wrote: *How do atheists convince themselves that they know things when they actually don't. The answer, surprisingly enough, has to do with a profound misunderstanding of science.* He illustrated this statement by a comical incident with Russian cosmonauts returning from the space mission. They searched space all over the place and found no God; thereby they triumphantly affirmed the atheistic doctrine to be true."

"Hah. That's very funny. This stuff is confusing the hell out of me. My head is spinning."

"I haven't even questioned the Secular Progressives about how such wonders as human consciousness, including our moral sense, language, mathematics, art, beauty, music, love, longing for immortality and soul ascent could be created by random mutation from nothing. Our future Intelligent Machines probably will never even touch any of these wonders.

In the mean time, no science in the world is more responsible for human suffering than the theory of evolution, as Ann Coulter is stating in her book 'Godless':

While relentlessly attacking God, the Darwin cult hides behind the claim that they are merely doing science... (But) theory of gravity has never been invoked to justify mass murder, genocide, or eugenics. Darwin's theory of evolution has. From Marx to Hitler, the men responsible for the greatest mass murders of the twentieth century were avid and outspoken Darwinists.

184

Hitler hated Judaism, the religion of 'sub-humans'. He hated Christianity too: 'It filled people's heads with silly, sentimental notion about helping the weak and infirm,' he said. He believed that the 'heaviest blow that ever struck humanity was the coming of Christianity'. Don't we find our radical Left solidly in bed with a very ominous crowd?"

"You're not really religious, Deda, but you sure sound like it. Do you actually believe in Intelligent Design in your heart and mind?"

"I'm still not religious in a traditional sense; but I love thinking as an enjoyable process; and I don't take bull-crap for granted any more. Forty five years behind the curtain is more than enough. At this point of debate and knowledge I'm just trying to make an intellectual choice. It's only natural for me to think that only the Deity or some other supernatural force would be capable of creating this universe of ours with such an incredible beauty, unimaginable precision and self-sustaining complexity. I've always admired intelligence; it feels nice to be surrounded by it. Real intelligence never makes you feel inferior. It lifts you with it, makes you part of it. I prefer to accept the idea of Intelligent Design; and if I ever find myself wrong, it would be perfectly fine—I've had some fun in the mean time."

185

"How do you imagine the Deity?

"I don't know. Maybe it's my lifetime spiritual handicap talking, but I don't have to imagine the Deity as a fierce old man depicted in the Sistine Chapel frescos, who is watching your every step and writing your name in the book of life. In fact, I would not visualize anything at all. I'd rather believed that upon completion of this omni-intelligent, and perfectly self-sustaining System, part of which we are, He left us alone with free will to make our choices and reap what we seed. Does my hypothesis sound too profane?"

"Confusing, maybe."

"Well, in one of his publications about relationship of science and religion, Albert Einstein said:

> *The interpretation of religion, as here advanced, implies a dependence of science on the religious attitude, a relation, which, in our predominantly materialistic age, is only too easily overlooked. While it is true that scientific results are entirely independent from religious or moral considerations, those individuals to whom we owe the great creative achievements of science were all of them imbued with the truly religious conviction that this universe of ours is something perfect."*

"Had Einstein called himself a Deist?"

"I don't recall; but if so, it's nice to be in a good company!"

"Strong stuff, Deda, and good food for thought, but why are you so harsh with atheists, considering your own limited religious fervor. Why wouldn't you just let them be?"

"I don't have anything against them and their freedom of expression, as long as they don't dictate what I am supposed to think. The Secular Progressives are the ones who are intolerant to other's beliefs. The Cross or a Nativity Scene displayed outside in holidays they consider an obscenity; the Ten Commandments displayed in public they regard as an insult. Religious freedom to me is a freedom to worship or not, wherever and whenever one wishes, as long as he doesn't force anyone else to participate or pay for it. This is exactly what our constitution means, and that's what I call a *fair game*."

"True enough! I'm exhausted. What is for tomorrow, Deda?

"Tomorrow is the last day of your vacation, Myron. How did you like our adventure?"

"Do you have to ask? "

*****

"Don't you wonder why I dumped this elemental political science on you?" I asked Myron on our way back to Vegas.

"Yes, I do. I admit it was informative and entertaining, but not quite elemental to my understanding. I just have to sort a lot of things out."

"Attention is the mother of retention, so to speak; and we do need a good retention of history in our memory. Think, Myron, of those radical Left zealots in Russia, who couldn't find a better application of their talents as to dedicate their lives undermining their Country's young democracy for the sake of Socialism, the most ridiculous and, as it is well proven, the ultimately evil social formation. Now turn around and look into the dark left corner of our society. Right there. Those few people sitting there are doing everything possible to do the same with their own Country, which according to Tyler is already in need of all the therapy it can get. Well, they don't have time to read history. They are too busy speaking."

"So, what you think these groups have in common, why are they so hungry for power?"

"Here, Myron, we come to the most interesting paradox of all: *Despite all liberal rhetoric, the radicalism is always profoundly antidemocratic.*"

"Why, Deda. Where is the logic?"

"Our Republic is based on rules of law, where majority defines this law and provides constitutional guarantees for the rights of minorities. Radicals of any sort are by definition in minority. When they are striving for power— and they often do—they circumvent democratic process and use any method, acting on the edge of legality and morality. It seems like *the common goal of the radical minority at any point in history has always been to control or even oppress the silent majority*. In the Soviet Union, in Nazi Germany, in Saddam's Iraq, and in today's Iran radicals succeeded in usurping the power for tangible periods of time. In Iraq and Afghanistan the radicals are making desperate effort to get their power back. Europe is now under brutal assault from Muslim immigrant minorities, threatening to swallow this original center of Western civilization. Even America isn't safe anymore"

"I still don't understand what benefits would Progressives derive from pushing their theory of Evolution on a forefront of the political dispute."

"Well, I believe, as a minority, progressives can't easily abolish or circumvent our Constitution in order to grab power. The Bolshevik's kind of revolution is hardly possible either. So they hope to achieve this goal by modifying American Constitution the *evolutionary* way, by creating a crisis after crisis and forcing the public to adopt some incremental changes. As long as they control the government, they hope to erode our Constitution to submission; and the pace of this process is accelerating now exponentially."

"You made me shiver, Deda."

"Now you know what the result of Bolshevik's effort in Russia was. Out of a phoenix of radical liberalism rose an ugly vulture of a new utopian society with its misery, slavery and death. Socialism often adapts some elements of a free society, just to survive; but its real enemy is Capitalism with its reliance on the power of individual, free market and democracy. Thus, the logic of the matter is: *The more power in the hands of the state, the closer is this structure to a Socialism, where the radical minority of any kind and color always rules.*"

"How does Islamism fit into your theory, Deda?"

"Shariah is the constitution of a global Islamic totalitarian state. The state power over Muslims and its judicial authority is absolute. The Muslim population is too often submitted to a radical theocratic minority, thoroughly brainwashed, and heavily dependent upon welfare, which is deliberately created and sustained."

"I can't fathom why the grown up Ivy League Professors or even some business moguls work for the demise of their own Country and prosperity like a bunch of Trotskyites of a hundred years ago."

"It's difficult to contemplate, Myron; but I think I found some explanation in the book of Dr. Dinesh D'Souza 'The Enemy at Home'. Dr. D'Souza has stated the reason for this paradox quite bluntly:

Since European decadence stands at the opposite pole to the traditional values of non-Western cultures, the Left is faced with the problem: how to impose the liberal values of Europe on those conservative cultures? To achieve a fundamental transformation of American foreign policy, the left needs America's current policy to suffer a loss from which it cannot recover. The Left seeks to engineer this defeat by imposing so many restraints (on America) that we can neither win the war abroad nor effectively defend against terrorist attacks at home. This strategy sets up a no-lose situation: it is the liberals who encumber us, yet it is us who will be blamed if there is another attack. The Left also tried to demoralize American people so that they demand immediate withdrawal from Iraq. This is where Jihad and the Iraqi insurgents come in (handy). The terror they produce is the propaganda the Left need in order to convince the American people that the war is imposing an unacceptably high toll. Even decapitation broadcasts over the Internet serves the purpose of disheartening Americans, which is why the Left shows no indignation over Al Qaeda's use of such tactics.

It looks like a diabolically clever strategy, Myron, the 'Leniniana' all over again. I told how Lenin manipulated WWI to grab power with bare hands. Lenin didn't care how many lives it would take in the worldwide war to achieve this goal. Stalin cared even less. It took Stalin over 50 million victims in Russia to promote his agenda."

"You like the political stand of Dr. D'Souza, don't you?"

"Well, D'Souza helped me to connect missing dots in my understanding of the radical Left positions on our war against radical Islam. They are in a minority and they are desperate for power. Just like Lenin and Trotsky in their maneuvering with war and peace, the land and bread, modern radical Left is playing political games on the very edge of treason. They think they can put an Islamic totalitarian Genie back in the bottle after they get power. It's like a bad dream all over again, in which Leon Trotsky was winning against the declining Russian Royal superpower and playing right into the hands of the greatest evil of all, the Totalitarianism."

"So, as I read you right, this is the working class paradise what your sucker Trotsky was fighting for. Should I, Deda, email him to ask what he thinks about the fate of his creation?"

"Call Lenin's Cell phone. You may find Trotsky nearby, probably in the same hell-cell. Some of their mates call it - the site of the *Permanent Celestial Revolution, or the Worldwide Dictatorship of Proletariat.*"

*****

It was monsoon time in this part of Arizona. The monsoon often brings a few days of torrential rains, when walls of water are rushing from the mountain ranges down thru the valley toward the Colorado River. The dry solid ground of the desert doesn't absorb this flood. The rushing water carves the surface with mini-canyon types of crevices and washes away everything in its path. The countless engineering systems of managing this flood are built in the "civilized" areas of the region to protect the roads and buildings. One of these systems, called appropriately *The Wash,* was built along and behind the rear border fence of my community. The Wash contains a cascade of reservoirs (ponds) overflowing from one to another below and delivering the floodwater into the Colorado River. A system of pumps is provided to empty the reservoirs from one to another below and to prepare them for the next rain. The dirt excavated during construction of these reservoirs formed the elevated plateaus along the Wash. My house was built on top of one of these plateaus, now an excellent observation point of the golf course being built right behind the Wash.

We were awakened early in the morning by loud desert thunder, rushed to the covered patio, and looked at the Black Mountain range in front of us. Rain formed a solid wall over the mountains, but hadn't reached us yet. The lightning looked like a continuous spider-web, touching the slopes. We could still see some stars above the house, but water was already rushing into the dry lake below, the first one in the system. This reservoir was filling up fast. The pumps had already started, and in fifteen minutes the reservoir was full, overflowing into the next. Another ten minutes -- and the thunderstorm was raving right above our house..

Epilogue

"How did you make out," Henry asked me when I was filling him in about my trip with Myron. "Did you have quality time with your bright young liberal?"

"Yes, Henry, we have had quite a productive trip, and I enjoyed it immensely. He was an excellent bouncing board; but I'm afraid, I've got him exhausted by my lecturing. Of course, I hope he understood that I just expressed my set of opinions, the philosophy of a new American in his humble perception.

As usual, Henry, the American West was beyond description, and I'm glad I had an opportunity to show my grandson how magnificent our great Country is. Besides, if my grandson is a liberal, I wish some young liberals would hold him as a role model.

This trip was a perfect setup for an open exchange of views. Myron has a good balanced personality and a mature outlook; he's easy to get along with. I'm looking forward to seeing him next summer. Maybe I'll buy him

Bose head-phones, so he can filter out junk of his noisy college environment. How do you like my manuscript, by the way?"

"I'm both impressed and depressed with the predictions and parallels in your book," he said. "I understand it's almost impossible to write a serious book about never changing values, while watching TV every day. I'm afraid, life is developing here much faster than you could imagine in your easygoing Canyon Land. Things you thought would never happen in our Country are already here. You are thinking that the idealistic maniac Leon Trotsky, the highly educated Chairman Lenin, and the Asiatic monster Stalin were bad. Well, now the very influential people like the White House communication director Anita Dunn are making speeches in high schools and other places advocating proletarian revolution and looking up to Chairman Mao, who starved, tortured and killed countless millions of his own citizens."

"I know, Henry; but I trust in the American ability to fight the challenging times. I realize, however, that there are too many people around who still need to be educated. I think Dr. Tyler had a clear vision of our current situation two hundred years ago; but our Country saved the world in the WWI, WWII, and the Cold War. She is ready to help when disaster strikes at any corner of the world. Her sacrifices have been indispensable (not necessarily appreciated) in war against global terror, poverty, violence, and other crap."

"That's right, buddy," echoed Henry with groan. "Whose sons and daughters are in Haiti now with the fully loaded warehouses shaped like *warplanes,* and floating hospitals and kitchens looking like warships. I just wonder, who will be accused in engineering and triggering of this earthquake, when dust settles?"

"You know the answer. I guess, we have to live with this asymmetry till day of judgment."

"No, thanks! On this subject, a concept of *redistribution* would suit me just right."

THE END